The Crescent in Clouds

The Crescent in Clouds

The Most Common Questions about Islam and Muslims Answered

AKHTARUL WASEY

SHIPRA

Rs. 995; US$ 40

ISBN: 978-93-88691-27-4

First Published in India in 2019

The Crescent in Clouds:
The Most Common Questions about Islam and Muslims Answered

Published by:
SHIPRA PUBLICATIONS
LG 18-19, Pankaj Central Market
I.P. Ext., Patparganj, Delhi 110092, India
Tel.: +91 11 2223 5152/6152, 9650028065
E-mail: info@shiprapublication.com
www.shiprapublication.com

Dedicated to
Mr. Hasan Nawaz Rahimtula

Foreword

This is the century of an unprecedented pace of change. It is also being characterised as the 'age of accelerations'. The preceding century witnessed great advances in science and technology, and successful global upsurge for the eradication of colonialism and imperialism. It also realized the urgency of global peace initiatives after having gone through the pain, agony and destruction of two World wars. It would be worthwhile to recall the global commitment from the Preamble of the UNESCO that came into force as early as November 4 of 1946: "*The Governments of the States Parties to this Constitution on behalf of their people declare: That since wars begin in the minds of men, it is in the minds of men that the defences of peace must be constructed.*" But where do we stand now? Is it not the mind of the man that has spread violence, insecurity, fundamentalism, bigotry and distrust around the globe? The human mind needs to be nourished on the right path during the years of growth of the child into adulthood. Every civilization has a well-established tradition of knowledge quest, its utilization and most importantly, its transfer to the generations ahead. Somewhere because of inadequacies in the discharge of this obligation, the world is not at peace with itself. There seems no respite in spite of sporadic preaching and pronouncements, assurances and agreements that assure every government and nation ready to contribute to create a world of peace, tranquillity, human dignity and equality of opportunity to one and all. Is it not really intriguing that never before, man had so much of knowledge and understanding of the forces of nature, the bounty of resources it offered for humanity, irrespective of any diversity? This is the age of knowledge power, mind power; of universal access to education and knowledge. Also, never before human beings had skills, mobility and connectivity to reach every human being, feed every mouth, ensure a hunger-free, dignified, healthy and decent life to every human being around the globe. In the world of such encouraging achievements, why are we not competent enough in achieving peace, cohesion and tranquillity across the globe? What is the pragmatic assessment of how global peace could really be established, and people could learn to live together? It is also realized that to move towards global peace and harmony, it is essential that people develop right comprehension of their own religion, and also accept the premise of the equality of all religions. The present effort by an eminent scholar Professor Akhatarul Wasey comes at the right moment, and in the right direction in putting the correct interpretation of Islam before people. His interpretations clearly elaborate how the existence of the diversity of all religions is necessary for human existence, as it educates people in the commonality amongst all religions.

In the changing context of widespread mobility of people of diverse socio-cultural, ethnic and religious background mingling, it is the mind of man that needs to be nourished and nurtured on the path of mutual respect for diversity that includes social cohesion and religious amity. Diversity of every conceivable variety; including that of social, cultural, ethnic, economic, linguistic, regional, and religious needs not just to be tolerated but sincerely accepted. It deserves to be respected, and celebrated. Logical and rational comprehension of religious diversity could play a great part in the human march towards global peace and harmony. While religions – their misinterpretations by vested interests – have led to violence and wars in the past, none can deny the civilizational contribution of every religion. It is the presence of different religions that has led to the advancement of human civilization and acceptance of common values. Every religion has encouraged the need to create and generate knowledge. Religion has become the most sensitive of the issues that often result in conflicts. The most important initiative towards a world of peace is to let every human being accept the equality of all religions. Right from initial years in schools, children must know the basics premises and philosophies of all religions. Children must know the commonalities, and also be made to respect the differences wherever these exist. The civilizational contributions of all religions; once made known to children; shall concretise their respect for all religions. Once they are aware of the commonalities, they would appreciate and respect the differences as well. Every religion accepts the basic values of Truth, Peace, Non-Violence, Righteous Conduct and love. These could become the corner stones of religious amity and social cohesion.

The book "The Crescent in Clouds: The Most Common Questions about Islam and Muslims Answered" by Prof. Akhtarul Wasey is a unique initiative to let people understand the basics of Islam; the Religion of Peace. He responds to queries from common man to enlightened citizens on various aspects of Islam. It reiterates, in a way, that if someone comprehends the basics of his religion truthfully, he would neither disrespect any other religion, nor hate or dislike their followers. Every child must be made familiar with the basics of all religions. An eminent scholar of international reputation, Prof. Wasey has responded to every query at the level of comprehension of the inquirer. Every answer indicates his in-depth knowledge of Islam, other religions, and also the common basic values. The queries are classified under the religious, social, political, economic, educational and miscellaneous chapters. It also emerges prominently in the responses that "*Seeking knowledge is the duty for every Muslim man and women*" and also that "*Angels spread their feather on the way of the seeker of knowledge.*" This book assists every seeker of the better understanding of Islam. Once someone understands the true philosophy of his religion, he is bound to become an effective contributor to the peaceful existence of all religions. Professor Wasey deserves all salutations and appreciation in presenting this volume for wider use and understanding.

Professor J.S. Rajput
Padma Shri Awardee
India Representative on the Executive
Board of the UNESCO

April, 2019

In the name of Allah, Most Compassionate, Most Merciful

Introduction

The Crescent in Clouds by a distinguished Muslim scholar of our time, Professor Akhtarul Wasey has many merits to recommend itself.

First, it is aptly titled. For it allays many misconceptions and misperceptions about Islam and Muslims. It succeeds remarkably in cleaning some nagging doubts about Muslim faith, practices, customs and rituals.

Next, this work displays truly the Islamic spirit of peaceful co-existence Professor Wasey stands out, in the light of his cogent answers to various provocative question, for his catholicity of mind and his deep regard for all faiths. More remarkably, he makes no compromise about the articles of Islamic faith. Such a balance and poise is generally conspicuous by its absence in most of the writings on faith.

Furthermore, the range of Professor Wasey's scholarship is breathtaking. He has addressed an array of questions related to doctrinal, polemical, political, social, spiritual and economics aspects of Islam and Muslims' lives. Far from betraying any sense of triumphalism or apologia, Professor Wasey has painstakingly and conscientiously resolved doubts, apprehensions and even loaded questions about some delicate, sensitive topics. In so doing, he keeps amazingly clear of any controversy or partisanship.

Professor Wasey's elucidation of things Islamic is destined to go a very long way in helping readers, Muslims and non-Muslims alike, in grasping the stance of Islam on a variety of issues.

The author has done a laudable, nay enviable job in projecting a sane, sensible and authentic image of Islam and Muslims, without causing offence to anyone. This work will be read with great profit by all those who are interested in gaining a deeper and broader knowledge of Islam in a reader-friendly format. This book is specially welcome in our times for in the emotionally surcharged atmosphere reeking of the global Islamophobia, such helpful books are very much needed for describing what Islam is and what it is not.

Professor Wasey's credentials as a scholar of Islamic studies are impeccable. The present work underscores his sincerity of purpose, his thorough grounding in Islam and his concern for constructing a world in which all religions enjoy respect and understanding. For these reasons the present work is bound to strike a chord in every heart.

Professor Abdur Raheem Kidwai
Ph.D. (Leicester, UK)
Director
K.A. Nizami Centre for Quranic Studies
Aligarh Muslim University, Aligarh

Aligarh
March 2019

Preface

We are presently living in the age of Islamophobia as Muslims have been under fire from all quarters across the world. The crescent of Islam is eclipsed by dark, menacing clouds.

This book is a compilation of questions and answers about Islam and Muslims, which were serialised every week in the early 2000s in the Hindi daily *Rashtriya Sahara* at the behest of its then editor, Shri Govind Dixit and his colleague Mr. Chand Rahmani. While I cannot pass any judgement on the impact of this series, which lasted for almost two years, I learnt much from the questions posed by readers. This helped me also in soul searching and analysis about Islam and Muslims.

The Hindi and Urdu versions of this book have already appeared from Bikaner and Delhi respectively. At the behest of my friends and well-wishers, especially Dr Muzaffar Hussain Syed, this English version has now been published. I regard this publication as a modest contribution to re-orienting the human mindset and understanding. We now live in a global village and it is incumbent upon everyone in the world to profess and practice the principle of peaceful coexistence and to forge cordial ties of mutual love and fraternity. Although we live together, we live separately, in isolation from others. One group or community does not know much about the other. This lack of communication breeds distrust. I think this series of questions will contribute to allaying some misperceptions and distrust. The mutual trust and understanding among various communities will pave the way for unity and solidarity not only in India, but also at every level in our global village. I am sure this book will strengthen mutual understanding and goodwill.

Certain topics and issues have to be tackled with great caution and sensitivity. It must be ensured that no statement should hurt the feelings of any group, especially their religious sentiments. Accordingly, no individual has been named in this book. In line with context, if someone is named, it is done in order to oppose a particular stance. We must stand up against every such stance, which is inimical to humanity, solidarity, scientific approach and the spirit of our Constitution. This should be considered as the rationale behind publishing this book.

The terms used in the book have been explained in the "Glossary" appended to the book in order to facilitate readers' understanding and comprehension.

Professor Akhtarul Wasey
Padma Shri Awardee
President
Maulana Azad University, Jodhpur and
Professor Emeritus (Islamic Studies)
Jamia Millia Islamia, New Delhi-110025

Acknowledgement

For the publication of this work in English, I stand indebted to the noted educationist Professor Dr. J. S. Rajput whose "Foreword" has enhanced the prestige of this work. I am grateful to the distinguished academician, Professor Abdur Raheem Kidwai, who has kindly contributed the "Introduction" to the book.

I fail to find words to thank my colleagues at the Departments of Islamic Studies and Hindi at Jamia Millia Islamia, Delhi, who helped me in their own ways in formulating my responses to the questions published in the daily *Rashtriya Sahara* (Hindi). They extended me useful cooperation in the compilation of the same question and answer series in book form in Urdu and Hindi.

Let me thank Dr. Ahmed Khan, my former colleague at the National Commission of Linguistic Minorities, and Mr. Parvez Ahmed, one of my associate at the Maulana Azad University, Jodhpur, for helping me in bringing out this book.

I would be failing in my duty if I do not thank Mr. D. Kumar, Managing Director of a leading publication house and his associates. Shipra Publications deserves credit for the appearance of this book to strengthen mutual understanding and goodwill.

Contents

Foreword by Professor J.S. Rajput vii
Introduction by Professor Abdur Raheem Kidwai xi
Preface xii
Acknowledgement xv

1. Religious Questions 1
2. Social Questions 73
3. Political Questions 102
4. Economic Questions 126
5. Educational Questions 128
6. Miscellaneous Questions 136

Glossary 155
Index 159

1
Religious Questions

Question: How many years did the revelation of the Qur'an take? What is the difference between Makkan and Madinah Surahs?

Answer: It took 23 years to reveal the Qur'an. The revelation of the Qur'an began with the declaration of the Prophethood of Muhammad (Pbuh) and lasted until he left for his heavenly abode. He was 40 years old, when his prophethood was conferred on him and he left for his heavenly abode at the age of 63. He lived in Makkah for thirteen years, after the proclamation of his prophethood and subsequently migrated to Madinah, where he lived for ten years. The Surahs revealed to him, during his stay in Makkah are called Makkan Surahs. Likewise, the Surahs revealed to him, during his sojourn in Madinah are called Madinah Surahs.

Question: Is it permissible for one to slaughter the sacrificial animals on the first day only after the performance of Eid-ul Azha prayer. Is it permissible for one who shares the sacrificial animal with others to slaughter it, while other shareholders have not yet performed Eid-ul Azha prayer?

Answer: Yes. It is permissible for one to slaughter the sacrificial animals only after the performance of Eid-ul Azha prayer.

Question: Allah sends blessings on His beloved Prophet Muhammad (Pbuh). What are his special contributions? Why is he regarded as the leader of the prophets? Why did Allah call him His 'beloved'?

Answer: Prophet Muhammad (Pbuh) is the last of the prophets and messengers of Allah. He combined in his ideal personality all meritorious qualities, sublime virtues and vital values possessed and represented by all the prophets and messengers, from Adam (a.s.) to Isa (a.s.). By virtue of his sincere practice of what he earnestly preached, he emerged as the most perfect model to be emulated. The structure of his teachings and the ideal way of his life, rest on the belief in Allah, His Oneness and undivided servitude to Him, maintenance of ties of kinship, propagation of love and affection, furtherance of harmony and peace and promotion of respect and reverence for the entire humanity. Most of these values have been appropriately stressed by the Qur'an.

Question: Can the goods used in one mosque be used in another mosque?
Answer: Spare goods of one mosque may be used in another mosque.

Question: There are about eight hundred Muslims in my village. They live in two separate localities. They perform Juma prayer in the mosques of their respective localities. However, most of the people assemble in the old mosque to perform Juma prayer. Is it proper to perform Juma prayer in two different mosques of the same village? Moreover, according to a resident Maulawi Sahab, it is not permissible for one to perform Juma prayer in a village mosque. In compliance with his instruction, Zuhr prayer is also performed after the performance of Juma prayer. Besides, the people pray obligatory cycles of Zuhr prayer in a congregation. Then they perform the rest cycles of prayers – sunnah (recommended prayers) and nafl (non-obligatory prayers) in consonance with the prescription of Zuhr prayer. Would you like to throw some light on these issues?
Answer: It is permissible to perform Juma prayer in two different mosques, situated in a big town or in a big village. On Fridays Zuhr prayer is prescribed only for a traveller and for those who have missed their Juma prayer, under some unavoidable circumstances. It is not obligatory for the women to perform Juma prayer. None other than these people are allowed to perform Zuhr prayer on Fridays.

Question: In an Islamic state, the hand of a thief is chopped off for his crime. With reference to the punishment meted out to him, is it permissible to perform the funeral prayer of a thief? What are the prescribed punishments for those who do not perform five daily prayers? Who, according to four Imams, can be branded as a non-votary of prayer?
Answer: It is permissible for us to perform the funeral prayer of a Muslim thief. Islam prescribes the punishment of chopping off of the hand of a convicted thief, not only as a measure to deter other thieves but also to purge the society of crimes. Chopping off of a hand of a convicted thief is a kind of penance for his crime. Notably, he is not subjected to death sentence. Therefore, a deceased thief is treated like a common deceased Muslim. There is a general consensus among all four Imams of jurisprudence that those, who deny the obligatory nature of prayer (Salah)

are out of the fold of Islam. One who is neglectful of prayers will be meted out with different types of punishments.

Question: It has been observed that some Sufis and spiritual guides indulge in dancing to Qawwalis. Someone has said, "This state is called 'wajd'." Can this dance be appropriately called 'wajd'?

Answer: Falling into an ecstatic trance during the Qawwali sessions, is integral to the traditions of shrines and mausoleums. It is an expression of the strong emotions and feelings to go into such trances after listening to the spiritual musical notes and deeply stirring compositions. Many Sufis met their Lord by virtue of falling into a deep trance.

Question: Sometimes, verses relating the story of Yusuf (a.s) and Zulaikha are recited during the performance of some prayer. Won't the recitation of such verses invalidate the prayer? Should votaries of prayer in their praying mode remember Allah or Yusuf (a.s) and Zulaikha?

Answer: It is permissible to recite any verse of the Qur'an during the performance of a prayer.

Question: The Qur'an is believed to have been sent down from the heavens. Can you name any Surahs which fire can't gut, water can't wash away and air can't erase?

Answer: Consisting of the final message of Allah, the Qura'n was revealed to His last Prophet and Messenger – Muhammad (Pbuh)—in deed a miracle sent down by Allah, the Qur'an remains intact with its distinctive characteristics. It has been well safeguarded against the corruption in memory as well as in writing that not even a single letter or a vowel point has been yielded to interpolation. This is the most widely read book, in the world. For instance, the votaries of prayer recite its verses in every cycle of prayer, five times a day. In Taraweeh prayer, the Huffaz leading prayer read out the entire Qur'an and the other votaries of the prayer listen to the verses attentively. Besides, there are millions of Muslims, who have learnt the entire Qur'an by heart. By virtue of these things its fire can't gut, the water can not wash it away and even the air can not erase any of its Surahs.

Question: According to the meaning of a prophetic tradition the period, when Allah allots the portion of livelyhood to His servants (men) is from the early dawn to the sunrise. It is clearly evident that those who are not awake during this period will be deprived of the portion allotted by Allah. However, it is quite common among the Muslims to sleep after the performance of Fajr prayer during the month of Ramadan. Aren't these people deprived of the portion allotted by Allah?

Answer: This famous prophetic tradition is relevant to our needs and betterment. Allah sends down His special gifts early in the morning. Moreover, early rising leads to sound physical health, religious advancement and social development. During the month of Ramadan, most of the Muslims stay awake at night for the sake of prayer and other forms of worship. Besides, they also get up during late night for their pre-dawn meal. This is the reason that some of them take rest after the performance of Fajr prayer.

Question: Would you like to throw some light on Masjid-ul-Aqsa situated in Palestine?

Answer: Built in Bait-ul-Maqdas or Jerusalem, a holy city, it is the place where Prophet Muhammad's (Pbuh) celestial journey (Me'raj) was broken. According to an Islamic belief, all the prophets and messengers of Allah assembled there and performed some prayer which was led by Prophet Muhammad (Pbuh).

Question: Whenever people asked Prophet Muhammad (Pbuh) the meanings of 'wahid' and 'ahad', he would answer, "Both words have the same meaning". How can two words—one singular and the other plural—can bear the same meaning?

Answer: No word, 'wahid' or 'ahad' is plural. Both are singular and are synonymous. They are used to indicate the attributive names of Allah. According to an Arabic lexicon, the plural of 'ahad' is 'ahaad'. The words 'wahid' and 'ahad' are translated as 'one', 'alone' and 'unique'. As regards 'wahid', it is an Arabic number, which means 'one'.

Question: Is Allah 'ahad' or 'wahid'?

Answer: Allah is 'ahad' as well as 'wahid'. Both words have the same meaning one or only one.

Question: Does lovemaking with one's spouse cause major uncleanliness or impurity? If the couple does not take off the clothes, during lovemaking; will the clothes be considered defiled? Do such clothes need be washed? Can the couple, following their obligatory major bath, wear these clothes to perform the prayer?

Answer: It is mandatory for the couple to have a major bath after lovemaking. It is forbidden for one to offer prayer, enter the mosque, touch the Qur'an or read it in the state of one's major uncleanliness. If there is some filthy substance on one's clothes, it is essential for one to remove it and obtain cleanliness by washing the area covered by the filth. But it is not essential for one to wash the whole clothes. If the clothes have no filthy substance on them, one can wear these clothes to perform the prayer.

Question: According to A. A Farooqui, the numerals 786 stand for Bismillah-hir-Rahman-ir-Rahim, while on the other hand Abdur Razzaq Mansuri holds 788 to represent Bismillah-hir-Rahman-ir-Rahim. The expression Bismillah-hir-Rahman-ir-Rahim consists of 21 letters. Every letter represents a certain number – ba: 2, seen: 60, meem: 40, alif: 1, ha: 5, alif: 1, lam: 30, ra: 200, ya: 8, meem: 40. The grand total is 788. If one writes the expression 'Harey Krishna' in Urdu and converts it into numerals, its grand total is 786. This expression may be represented in numeral as follows: ha: 5, ra: 200, ya: 10, kaaf: 20, ra: 200, sheen: 300, nun: 50, alif: 1. The grand total is 786. Which of these do you think is correct?

Answer: There is no general consensus, among the scholars regarding 786, which is commonly believed to represent the expression Bismillah-hir-Rahman-ir-Rahim. According to a group of the scholars of Islam, there are two vowel points (khada zabars) after first 'laam'. These vowel points have been wrongly counted as two 'alifs' by you. If you do not count them as 'alifs', the grand total is 786. The numerals 786 also represent 'Harey Krishna'. One can establish similitude in several other things, if one makes unstinted efforts.

Question: Can you trace the origin of the practice of wearing skull caps or other coverings on heads, during prayer? Is it not permissible to offer prayers without wearing any sort of head coverings?

Answer: The Muslims have been wearing skull caps and headgears (amamahs), since the days of the Prophet (Pbuh). They have been performing the prayers with their heads covered. However, the Prophet (Pbuh) has also been reported to have offered the prayers without his head coverings. A votary of prayers can, therefore, perform the prayers without the head coverings.

Question: Can Ihram be synonymous with shroud?

Answer: You have rightly grasped the underlying significance of wearing Ihram. I deem it appropriate to mention here that people with different traditions of dresses and garments wear Ihram, two unstitched sheets of cloth, obliterating the difference between the haves and have-nots. It presents a unique model of equality.

Question: My mother had affirmed the intention to perform the pilgrimage to holy House of Allah before her death. Now if her son performs the pilgrimage to the holy House of Allah on her behalf, would this obligatory duty due upon her be considered to have been fulfilled?

Answer: You can well perform Hajj on her behalf. You can also nominate some other virtuous Muslim to perform Hajj on her behalf.

Question: An Islamic scholar possesses so many costly books. If he sells them, he can get as much money as he requires for meeting the expenses of his journey to Makkah. Is the performance of Hajj incumbent on him?

Answer: The books of a scholar are for academic purpose. It is not at all proper for any one to declare Hajj obligatory for him even if he can get as much money, as he needs to undertake his journey to Makkah. According to Islamic jurisprudence, Hajj is not obligatory for those whose essential items if sold, may bring them as much money as they require for undertaking the pilgrimage to the holy House of Allah.

Question: What is the difference between Hajj and Qurbani? Is Hajj falling on a special day called Hajj-e-Akbar? Which is that special day? Are there any determined beliefs that Hajj after some particular years will be called Hajj-e-Akbar?

Answer: There are different opinions about Hajj-e-Akbar: (i) The day when the sacrificial animals are slaughtered, (ii) The day when the people performing Hajj gather on the plain of Arafat (iii) when Hajj falls on Friday (iv) wearing Ihram to perform Hajj on the prescribed days, during the month of Zil Hijj is called Hajj-e-Akbar and wearing Ihram for performing minor pilgrimage, is called Hajj-e-Asghar.

Question: Which of the two holy places – Makkah and Madinah, is more important for a Muslim?

Answer: Both Makkah and Madinah are the most important symbols of Islam and Islamic beliefs. Makkah enjoys a distinctive position, in the canon of Islam, because the first house of Allah for His worship was built there by Adam (a.s.), a messenger of Allah. The house of worship came to be known as Kaba. Then, Hazrat Ibraheem (a.s.) rebuilt it on the same foundation. Makkah enjoys a special place further, as Prophet Muhammad (Pbuh), the mercy for the world, was born here. Thirdly, the revelation of the holy Qur'an began here. The city of Makkah also boasts of the place, where Hazrat Ibraheem came to drop Hazrat Hajra and baby Ismaeel (a.s.) in compliance with Allah's command. And after all the city is also blessed with having the places, where the pilgrims go for the obligatory observance of Hajj. Similarly, Madinah, previously known as Yethrib, enjoys significant status in the canon of Islam. The people of Madinah had not only invited the Prophet (Pbuh) and his companions, during their tough times, but also preferred them over their relatives. They had fostered such a bond of relationship, which is still cited as an example par excellence. Secondly, the holy mausoleum of the Prophet (Pbuh) is here. And it was also the capital of the first Islamic state. Every Muslim pays a visit to the mausoleum of Prophet Muhammad (Pbuh) before or after the performance of Hajj. Thus, both the places with their distinct merits are revered most by all Muslims.

Question: What is the meaning of Hajj? Why is it performed? What are the obligatory observances of Hajj?

Answer: Literally the word 'Hajj' means 'intention or affirming intention'. In the terminology of Shariat, it means affirming one's intention to pay the pilgrimage to the holy house of Allah, situated in Makkah, in Kingdom of Saudi Arabia. An obligatory duty, Hajj is performed on the prescribed days with the prescribed basic rituals and obligatory observances. Kaba is the Qiblah, the point to which every votary of prayer faces. Hajj is an obligatory duty to be performed once in lifetime by those adult Muslims who can afford to undertake the journey to Makkah. Five daily congregational prayers, Friday prayer and prayers performed on the occasions of two festivals (Eidain) denote unity and brotherhood of the people of a locality, localities and of a city respectively. Likewise, Hajj, a yearly assembly of the Muslims, is the symbol of the unity of human beings and Islamic fraternity of the Muslims of the entire world.

Question: According to Islamic belief the performance of Hajj washes off one's sins. A rich person can perform Hajj and have his/her sins washed off. How can a poor Muslim be blessed with the rewards and virtues earned by the performance of Hajj?

Answer: Allah sent down Islam for the entire mankind. Of course, it goes without saying that human beings are naturally prone to mistakes. Allah, the Most Kind and Merciful, forgives the sins of His slaves in return of their deeds liked by Him. It is believed that one whose pilgrimage to the holy house of Allah is accepted by Him is blessed with His forgiveness. One may conveniently say that those whose pilgrimage to Makkah is accepted by Allah wisely avoid sins after the performance of Hajj. But Allah is under no compulsion to give one rewards for Hajj. Besides, it is not compulsory that every Hajj is accepted. As for poor Muslims, Hajj has been made subject to the condition by Allah. It is not incumbent upon those Muslims who do not have necessary means and ability. There are other, modes of worship for such Muslims to earn the rewards of Hajj.

Question: What is Kaba? If it is the house of Allah, why aren't the people of other beliefs allowed to visit it? During the lifetime of the Prophet of Islam, everyone visited this house of Allah.

Answer: Kaba, situated in Makkah, is the House of Allah. Those who believe in Allah and the prophethood of Muhammad (Pbuh) reserve every right to pay the pilgrimage to this house. And those who do not believe in Allah and His prophet obviously need not go there. It is a place of worship. It is not a tourist spot. Notably, it was the Prophet himself who prohibited the non-believers to visit this sacred house.

Question: What is 'Sang-e-Aswad'? Does the act of kissing it washes one's sins off? Does its colour changes, as many times as one kisses it? Who had brought it and fixed it there?

Answer: According to an Islamic belief, it is a stone brought from heaven. It was kissed by the Prophet Muhammad (Pbuh). Hence, the pilgrims to the house of Allah kiss it in consonance with the Prophetic tradition. Sang-e-Aswad (Black Stone) is not blessed with the power to safeguard one against any sins. It is none but Allah, who forgives the sins of a believer. So, every Muslim makes an attempt to attain Allah's pleasure and seek His forgiveness according to the ways prescribed by Allah and His Prophet. As regards the colour of the stone, it remains unchanged. It is as black as it was when Prophet Muhammad (Pbuh) had fixed it.

Question: What does the act of throwing seven pebbles at each stone pillar mean? Does this act really ensure Allah's refuge from the Satan?

Answer: Stoning the pillars is a symbolic act of rejecting the evil. The Satan appeared before Hazrat Ibraheem to mislead and prevent him from carrying out the command of Allah, *i.e.*, slaughtering his son Hazrat Ismaeel. In obedience to his father's order Hazrat Ismaeel threw pebbles at Satan so that he could ward him off.

Question: Generally, the financial conditions of the Muslims are not good. The pilgrims to the house of Allah have to spend a lot of money to meet the expenditure of Hajj. Isn't it possible that poor Muslims are permitted to undertake a free pilgrimage to the holy house of Allah?

Answer: An obligatory duty, Hajj has been made subject to some conditions. It is an incumbent duty for those adult Muslims who have the required means and ability. Needless to mention, before affirming one's intention for paying the pilgrimage to the holy house of Allah, one has to ensure that one is in no debt to anyone. At the same time, it is also important for one to ensure that one has surplus resources to provide for the expenses of one's dependent members in the family, after one undertakes the journey to Makkah. It is pertinent to mention that it is not obligatory on a poor Muslim to perform Hajj. Those Muslims who have necessary means, may nominate some virtuous Muslims to perform Hajj on behalf of their deceased, disabled or sick parents or other relatives. But there is no such organisation or institution which can bear the entire expenses of a poor pilgrim to travel to the holy house of Allah.

Question: If one day the graveyards all over the world come have no place for the deceased, where will then the deceased be buried?

Answer: This situation is impossible to arise because the old graves are levelled for the burials. But if there is a graveyard where all the graves have brick or stone structure around them, people will require another plot of land for the graveyard.

Question: Are the moon and stars stand considered as some religious symbols like Swastik insignia? If yes, what do they stand for?

Answer: I do not know whether Swastik is a religious or social symbol. As regards the moon and stars, these have no relationship with Islamic beliefs. Of course, these are regarded by people as the symbol of light, growth and development.

Question: I read in a Sunni Jantree that Allah did not like His slaves' act of sleeping on a Friday between first Azan and the prayer, between Maghrib and Isha prayers and also after Fajr prayer until the sunrise, without ablution. Can you substantiate it in the light of some Hadith (prophetic traditions)?

Answer: One may conveniently substantiate it with the prophetic tradition in the light of which Islamic scholars consider the act of sleeping during the times mentioned in the question undesirable. But it is not Haram, or a forbidden act.

Question: Do the practising Muslims consider it unlawful to keep idols? Is the act of keeping idols considered as a form of idol worship? Isn't it narrow-mindedness?

Answer: There are a few Muslims who make idols, as also a few who keep them in their houses. Since Islam does not allow idol worship, the Muslims normally avoid making as well as keeping idols. It is a matter, strictly related to the belief, so it won't be fair to term a staunch Muslim as a narrow-minded person.

Question: In compliance with Allah's command, Hazrat Ibraheem (a.s.) had decided to sacrifice his son Hazrat Ismaeel (a.s.). Why don't the Muslims slaughter their sons, as the sacrificial offerings to Allah? I put the same question to the worshipper of Kali, a goddess, "Why don't they slaughter the devils in place of animals as sacrificial offerings?

Answer: Whatever Hazrat Ibraheem did, was in perfect harmony with Allah's good pleasure. In obedience to the order of Allah, he took his son for the sacrifice. But what he slaughtered came actually to be one of the animals prescribed for sacrifice. Muslims slaughter the prescribed sacrificial animals on prescribed days in compliance with Allah's command, as also in commemoration of Hazrat Ibraheem's willingness and readiness to sacrifice his son. Since I am not an authority on other religions, I can't comment on their practices.

Question: The Hindustani words 'tum' and 'tu' are plural and singular respectively. Why do the scholars of Islam use the plural pronoun and an auxiliary verb 'hain' (are) for Allah in their addresses? For example, they say, 'Allah farmatey hain' (Allah says). Conversely, Allah wishes His slaves to address Him as 'tu' and wants His beloved Prophet Muhammad (Pbuh) to be addressed as 'aap'. Will you elucidate?

Answer: The issue basically pertains to the linguistic difference between Arabic and other languages. But the word 'tum' is both singular and plural. It becomes plural when the words 'log' or 'sub' are added with it. For example, 'tum log / tum sub'. So, both 'tum' and 'tu' are used as singular pronouns. Usually people use the word 'tu' for Allah. However, some people also address Him with another word 'aap'. Both the addresses are proper.

Question: The holy graves of Hazrat Imam Husain is in Iraq. But some Muslims make raised platforms for symbolic models of Imam Husain's tomb. They also prepare a special dish called 'khichda' and desert called 'malida' on a particular occasion. They read out some verses from the

Qur'an placing these dishes in front of them. This practice is commonly called 'fateha'. Are the Sunni Muslims permitted to follow these practices? What are the injunctions in the light of the Qur'an and Hadith?

Answer: One can't substantiate it by the prophetic traditions because Prophet Muhammad (Pbuh) had left for heavenly abode years before the martyrdom of Imam Husain. It was the most tragic event in the history of Islam. As regards the Sunni scholars of Islam and the scholars of other Islamic schools of thoughts, you had better consult the scholars of your preference and choice.

Question: It is said, if the ankles of the votaries of prayer are covered by the length of their trousers, pants, etc., their prayer will become invalid. But I have seen some Imams wearing socks during their prayers. Aren't their prayers invalid?

Answer: It is not allowed for a Muslim to cover his ankles by the length of his trousers whether or not he is in the state of prayer. Some prophetic traditions strictly warn the believers against covering the ankles by the length of the trousers. In fact, it leads one to be puffed up with pride – a cause of one's damnation. Prophet Muhammad (Pbuh) wanted the Muslims to be purged of pride and arrogance and win Allah's pleasure by virtue of their various daily acts. As regards wearing the socks, one can perform one's prayers with socks. Prophet Muhammad (Pbuh) performed prayers while wearing socks.

Question: Who is to be branded as a Kafir? Is it permissible to give the meat of a sacrificial animal to the Hindus?

Answer: Literally the word '*Kafir*' means 'one who conceals'. In Islamic terminology, the word '*kafir*' refers to a person who does not believe in the Oneness of Allah and His perfect attributes. It also stands for those who do not believe in Allah in consonance with Islamic belief and injunctions. Moreover, one is called a *kafir*, because one denies the greatest truth, and also conceals it in spite of his knowledge about it. According to the Hindu belief, such people are branded irreligious or people without religion. As for the meat of a sacrificial animals, it can be given to Hindus or other non-Muslims, who eat meat.

Question: Will one's wife be considered to have been divorced, if one utters the word 'talaq' three times in one's state of anger, though without any one else to bear witness? Or, will it require three months' time? If a verbal divorce is given by the mutual consent of the husband and wife, when will the prescribed period of seclusion (Iddat) start? If a woman is on family way, will then the divorce be valid?

Answer: According to a prophetic tradition, divorce is the most detestable permissible act in the sight of Allah. One should try one's level best to wisely avoid it. One can go for it only when there is no other better option left to maintain the relationship. In case one is compelled to divorce one's wife, one is required to strictly follow the ways prescribed by Islam. According to Hanafi, Shafaee, Maliki and Hambali schools of jurisprudence divorce is deemed valid even if it is given in the state of anger. But according to Salafi scholars (*Ahl-e-Hadees*), another school of thought, divorce uttered for three times in one sitting is regarded as one divorce. It means the relationship between husband and wife is revocable. Notably, a divorced woman is not allowed to enter into another marriage until she passes three menstrual cycles during the prescribed period. In case a divorced woman is through the menopause, the prescribed period is for three Islamic calendar months. This period is prescribed to ensure whether or not a divorced woman carries the fetus of her previous husband. If a woman is divorced during her pregnancy, the prescribed period lasts till the delivery only. Divorce can be pronounced even if a woman is on family way.

Question: If the pervious husband of a woman wants to remarry her after the divorce, the woman is required to marry some other man and get divorced by him. Isn't it a mental torture inflicted on a woman for no fault of hers?

Answer: Islam does not allow the believers to force a woman or a girl to enter into marriage with one whom she does not like. As for Halala – the process of remarrying one's wife after divorce—pre-fixed Halala is not a prescribed way. It is not permissible for a pervious husband or the pervious wife to arrange a marriage where the woman will live for two-three days and later on she will be divorced by the present husband for the sake of a fresh marriage with the previous husband. Such people have been branded as non-grata by the Prophet (Pbuh). However, a situation can arise when the woman is left alone after the death of her second husband, then she can marry her pervious husband.

Question: If a man utters the word 'talaq' three times by mistake or deliberately, and then he wants to revert to his wife, what are the Islamic injunctions regarding it?

Answer: Divorce is not a matter to be taken casually. One's mistake may lead to the termination of the bond of marriage. If a husband happens to utters 'talaq' three times, his wife stays divorced. If he wants to remarry her immediately, he is not allowed for it. Moreover, you can consult a Mufti (a scholar of Islamic Sharia) for detailed knowledge about it.

Question: According to a Fatwa (Islamic Verdict), it is not in consonance with Islamic laws to pronounce the word 'talaq' three times in one sitting for the termination of the bond of marriage. But, according to the four Imams 'talaq' pronounced three times in one sitting will terminate the bond of marriage. Which one is the correct way?

Answer: The Qur'an has explicitly prescribed the procedure of divorcing one's wife and there is a common consensus among scholars of Islam on this matter. The divorce will be considered valid, if one pronounces the word 'talaq' three times in a single sitting. This sort of divorce is called 'talaq-e-Mughullaza' or 'talaq-e-Bidat'. In fact, this method of pronouncing divorce came into practice with a sincere aim to safeguard the woman against constant persecution of the husband, for the husband can go on perpetrating cruelties on his wife after pronouncing the word 'talaq' once. Of course, it has been a much debated subject. All India Personal Law Board, which represents all the Muslims has been entrusted with the responsibility of taking the decision in this respect.

Question: The Muslim husbands do not provide subsistence allowance fixed by the Supreme Court on a plea of the absence of such directions in the Qur'an. According to the land abolition act, women are not given their share in the land and property of their parents. Why do the Muslims follow the ruling regarding land abolition act, whereas it is against the Islamic Sharia? Why does not Muslim Personal Law Board raise its voice against it?

Answer: It is an important issue. The Muslims deny subsistence allowance to their divorcees, but they agree to give the subsistence allowance for a limited period called Iddat. As for portioning the share to the women in the property of their parents, they are deprived of it as per the land abolition act. When the law was passed, the Muslims were in critical situation, facing the cataclysmic event of partition. They were struggling for the safety of their lives. This is the reason that they could not oppose this law. In view of their adverse conditions, they can't be blamed. But it is incumbent on the Muslim Personal Law Board to make serious democratic efforts towards the restoration of women's rights. It is in direct opposition to the command of the Qur'an to deny these rights to the Muslim women.

Question: Why is the word 'talaq' called 'talaq'? It causes separation, why at all is it permissible? In case a married woman needs to terminate the bond of marriage with her husband, what should she do? Why is it that only males have been given the right to divorce? Won't the husbands misuse their rights and subject their wives to cruelties? Aren't the women not prone to undue suffering? If given rights, women would have been able to protect themselves against the cruelties perpetrated on them by their husbands. The girls' consent is sought before being given into marriage. In the same manner, their consent should also be sought before divorcing them. Why is divorce deemed proper only after the pronouncement of the word 'talaq' by husbands? Elucidate in the light of the Qur'an and Hadith.

Answer: The word 'talaq' literally means 'freedom'. In terminology of Islamic Sharia, it refers to the termination of the bond of marriage. According to the meaning of a Hadith talaq is the most detestable permissible act in the sight of Allah. It is permissible only when the spouses are not able to live together in a cordial atmosphere due to certain valid reasons. They are permitted to terminate their marriage contract in order to live separately in a better way in consonance with the Islamic Sharia. Besides, Islam guarantees the right of Khula—release from the contract of marriage, for women. If husband and wife are not able to live together and the husband is not ready to divorce, her it is permissible for the wife to seek the release from the marriage in a way prescribed by Islam. As regards husbands' perpetration of cruelties on women, Islam is not to be held responsible. It is the responsibility of an individual to conduct himself well with his wife. The Qur'an and the Prophetic traditions arm us with virtues to conduct ourselves well for everybody and ensure justice to them, and also grant them their rights. If someone does not abide by Allah and His Messenger's commands, he transgresses the bounds set by them. Needless to say, transgression brings dire consequences for one.

Question: Can a Sunni boy and a Shia girl be lawfully married? What is the duration of iddat prescribed for a woman mourning her husband's death? How many wives can a Muslim have at a time?

Answer: Since both Sunni and Shia are Muslims, Sunni and Shia boys and girls are permitted to enter into marriage. The widow of a deceased husband has four months and ten days, as iddat period. But the iddat period for a divorced woman with menopause is for three Islamic calendar months. In case the woman is on family way, the iddat period in both cases will be till the birth of the child. Iddat refers to that period when the woman is confined to her house. She is not allowed to marry during this period. According to Islamic laws, no Muslim is allowed to have more than four wives at a time. It is pertinent to mention that Islam permits a Muslim male to marry the second woman under some special circumstances, but with stringent conditions.

Question: Hazrat Adam was made of clay. Every human being, even Bhagwan will die one day or the other. The Prophets like Adam (a.s) and Prophet Muhammad (Pbuh) entered into marriages and had their families. They shouldered the household responsibilities. Then, why do the followers Prophet Muhammad (Pbuh) use the expression 'Aap ne duniya se parda kar liya' (he left for heavenly abode) for Prophet Muhammad?

Answer: According to Islamic beliefs, Allah (whether you call Him Ishwar or Bhagwan) will never die. He has been existing since the eternity and will exist forever. Everyone believes that the prophets like other human beings were made of clay. All living creatures must die one day or the other. As for expression 'Aap ne duniya se parda kar liya' (he left for heavenly abode), the Muslims use it to accord reverence to Prophet Muhammad (Pbuh).

Question: I met with a road accident. I sustained a severe backbone injury and I am bed ridden. How can I perform Salah and observe fast in such a condition?

Answer: Whatever condition you are in you can pray—a symbolic Salah. If you can perform ablution it is well and good. In case you are not able to do so, you can perform dry ablution (Tayyamum) with a clean dry piece of clay. If you have not been advised by the doctor to skip fasts, you can fast provided that your fasting will not aggravate your illness.

Question: A section of Muslims oppose Fateha. What are your views?

Answer: The greatest advantage of Fateha is that rich Muslims have good food to distribute among the poor.

Question: There is a person. He performs Zuhr prayer instead of Juma prayer on Fridays, just because he presumes that it is not Friday today. And he comes to know that in fact it was a Friday only after missing the Friday prayer, what should he do now?

Answer: Juma prayer is obligatory. If, by mistake, someone performs Zuhr prayer in place of Friday prayer, he has to perform Friday prayer if the time of Friday prayer has not passed. It is pertinent to mention here that

Friday prayer is not obligatory for women and for those who are on a journey.

Question: If a votary of prayer sneezes during the prayer, should he continue the prayer?

Answer: Since the sneezing does not invalidate the prayer he should continue it.

Question: For furtherance of communal harmony and brotherhood, a Muslim leaves a will that his dead body should be burnt or it should be bathed in water of river Ganga before it is buried. Can his last will of his be considered in conformity with the Islamic belief?

Answer: No, it cannot be considered in consonance with Islamic belief and prescribed burial rites.

Question: If a Muslim comes to India from an Arabian country, where he had begun fasting one day before the Muslims in India; will he celebrate Eid on the day it will be celebrated in Arabian countries or on the day, it will be celebrated in India?

Answer: If a Muslim comes from an Arabian country during the month of Ramazan he will celebrate Eid on the day it will be celebrated by the Muslims in India. However, he has already fasted for 30 days, he will fast no more because the maximum number of days of fasting are thirty.

Question: Suppose a Hindu enters the fold of Islam, can he recite a few verses of the Qur'an with an intention to send the rewards of his recitation to the departed souls of his Hindu ancestors?

Answer: According to Islamic belief, everyone will be held responsible for his deeds. If someone embraces Islam, he automatically feels concerned about his non-Muslim ancestors and other relatives. But it won't be proper for him to adopt any methods against their religion.

Question: Can love between a man and a woman be accorded the status of one's love for Allah?

Answer: It is said that one can reach Allah by virtue of human love and service provided that the love is free from lust. The love-relationship, between a man and woman can lead to social immoralities and beget several other problems. In sum, the love and service of human beings is itself a sort of worship.

Question: Prophet Muhammad (Pbuh) commanded the Muslims to invoke Allah's blessing on him after the pronouncement of his name. The practice of writing 'Pbuh' is indicative of it. Is it proper for a prophet to command his followers to invoke Allah's blessing on him?

Answer: Of course, Prophet Muhammad (Pbuh) does not need anybody's invocation of Allah's blessing on him. He (Pbuh) came to the human beings as a redeemer of humanity. He enlightened people steeped in ignorance with the Divine message, ended superstitions, warned the heedless ones, guided the erring people, caressed the neglected and the oppressed, women and orphans and so on. He reformed the society, eradicated animalism, waged war against evil and set the people on the right path. He taught them about the rights of every creature and showed them the way to be in a perfect harmony with Allah and His laws. In view of his innumerable service to human beings as well as other creatures. Of course, one must invoke Allah's blessing on the prophet. In fact, it is for one's benefit only.

Question: I have come to know through some sources that the dead bodies of those who die during their Hajj are put in front of the Imam and funeral prayer is performed over there in Harem. What is surprising is that the Imam does not ensure whether the deceased is a male or female, an adult or a child. Tell me whether the Imam turns his head only the right side in order to terminate his obligatory prayer? Why doesn't he raise his hands for supplication?

Answer: The funeral prayer of the deceased male or female, adult or child can be performed together at a time. According to my knowledge, the Imams of both the holy mosques terminate the prayers by turning their heads right as well as left. They also raise their hands to supplicate. Nevertheless, it is pertinent to mention here that it is also in consonance with the prophetic traditions to terminate the prayer by turning one's head only right side. Similarly, it is also in compliance with the prophetic tradition to supplicate without raising hands. It is very important to supplicate to Allah after prayer but it is not an integral part of the prayer.

Question: If a married woman gives birth to a child only six months after her marriage; will the child be legitimate or illegitimate? Who will look after the child after the death of his parents?

Answer: A child born to a lawfully married mother is legitimate even if he is born after six months of the marriage. In the event of the parents' death, the new born child will be looked after by his maternal grandmother before he attains the age of majority.

Question: There are some people, who perform all the five daily prayers and observe fast during the month of Ramazan. But they hurl abuse at others, exchange hot words and come to blows on petty issues in their actual life situations. Can they be really called religious people?

Answer: If one is a regular votary of prayer and performs other acts of worship but there is no marked improvement in his moral behaviour and he does not observe social etiquettes, he needs to be more sincere and perform his acts of worship with total loyalty and devotion to Allah. But he cannot be branded as irreligious on account of his habit of mouthing foul words and indulging in fights.

Question: Islam does not give preferential treatment to people on the basis of colour, race, caste and language. Why is it then obligatory to recite the Qur'an in Arabic? For that matter, Allah understands the language of every living creature. He accepts the prayer delivered in any language.

Answer: No doubt Allah understands not only the languages of people but also their emotions and innermost desires. Colour, race, caste and languages are not the reasons of someone's getting preferential treatment. Muslims recite verses of the Qur'an in the Arabic language during five daily prayers as well as other prayers because Qur'an was revealed in the Arabic language. But scholars do encourage people to read the Qur'an with its translations in their mother tongues. Prophet Muhammad (Pbuh) recited the way it was revealed to him and his companions recited the way it was recited by him. So, the Muslims all over the world recite it as it was recited by them. It is quite relevant to mention that not even a single letter of the Qur'an has yielded to corruption. This is Allah's Book revealed for the guidance of entire human beings in the world. Its relevance is beyond time and space. As regards, its translation, no translation can claim for sure that this is what Allah meant by such and such verses. All the translations are, irrespective of language, human attempts to understand the intention and meaning of Allah's words and messages.

Question: According to the basic articles of Islamic belief, every deceased person will be resurrected on the last day. And they will be sent to heaven and hell according to their deeds in their probationary life on this earth. Will universe be disintegrated after the last day? Will the previous creatures be also brought back to life?

Answer: The Muslims are required to believe in the angles, the divine books, the messengers of Allah and in the day of resurrection. On the Day of

Judgement, everybody will have to give the account of his deeds to Allah. He will be rewarded for his good deeds and punished for the bad ones.

Question: What is 'tasbih'? Is it synonymous to the rosary beads used by the Hindus? When was it first used?

Answer: Literally the word 'tasbih' means singing the glory of Allah. Earlier some people used their fingers and some used seeds of dates for this purpose. Later on people started using beads of rosaries. It is a fact that people of other religions like Hinduism and Christianity also use them for the recitation of chosen words, as per their faith and belief. Normally, tasbihs possessed by the Muslims have one hundred beads in them.

Question: What is the difference between Qur'an and Hadith? It is said that the Qur'an is one of Allah's Books and it was revealed to Prophet Muhammad (Pbuh). It is also believed that whatever the Prophet (Pbuh) said was basically Allah's revelation to him. How can then one differentiate between the Qur'an and Hadith?

Answer: A book of perspicuous light and guidance for the entire humanity, the Qur'an in its entirety was revealed to Prophet Muhammad (Pbuh). It is still intact in its pristine form. The term 'Hadith' refers to sayings and doings of Prophet Muhammad (Pbuh), and also his silent approbation of the acts of his companions. Hadith and the verses of the Qur'an agree together. In other words, Hadith is basically the first interpretation of the Qur'an. In sum, Qur'an is the primary source of the Islamic laws, whereas Hadith is the secondary source.

Question: The weather is cloudy or hazy. A fasting Muslim (by confusion) breaks his fast before the sun set. What should he do after he comes to know the mistake?

Answer: Though he does not have to expiate for it, he has to compensate it by fasting next year during the month of Ramazan.

Question: The Muslims claim that the Qur'an was revealed to Prophet Muhammad (Pbuh). If one looks at *Surahs, Al-hamd* and *Qul huwallah,* closely one finds that everything has been said on behalf of human beings. Is it correct that some parts of the Qur'an are from human beings, as well?

Answer: Last of the heavenly Books, the Qur'an was revealed to Prophet Muhammad (Pbuh). It remains intact in its entirety. Not even a single letter has yielded to corruption. No human being has made any contribution towards the creation of the Qur'an. These two *Surahs – Al-*

Fateha and *Al-Akhlas*, are like the moral lessons imparted to the children by their parents and by masters to their disciples. Here, Allah teaches His slaves how to sing the glory of their Lord and how to supplicate. The expression '*Alhamdulillah*' implies both singing prays to Allah and exercising thankfulness to Him. If you look at the first word '*Qul*' of the other Surah '*Al-Akhlas*' which means 'say', you will realise that the slaves are taught by their Lord.

Question: Why are Muslim males prohibited from wearing silk clothes and golden jewelleries?

Answer: Muslim males are prohibited from using these things because they are the sources of exhibitionism, expression of pride and arrogance. More importantly, these do not fit well for males.

Question: Festivals imply happiness and festivities. Moharram is the occasion of sorrows and the Muslims do not wish happy Moharram to one another. Why is it at all called festival?

Answer: There are only two festivals in Islam: Eid-ul-Fitr and Eid-ul Azha. Other so-called festivals celebrated by the Muslims in India are in consonance with the Indian tradition. The month of Moharram occupies an important place, because of the martyrdom of Hazrat Imam Hussain (a.s.) – the grandson of Prophet Muhammad (Pbuh). Muslims commemorate the martyrdom of Imam-e-Hussain during the month of Moharram. So, there arises no question of celebration and wishing happy festival to one and other.

Question: Are Sufis committed to the Islamic tenets? If they abide by Islamic laws, then what is the difference between *Shariat* and *Tareeqat*?

Answer: Sufism strictly propagates the belief that no one can ignore or transgress the bounds set by Islamic laws. One who transgresses or tends to transgress is not entitled to be called a Sufi in the strict sense of its meaning. Our close study reveals the facts that a Sufi observes the Islamic laws more strictly than Aalims, Qazis and Muftis. Qazis and Muftis give the verdict on the basis of the external deeds. While on the other hand, Sufis stress the need of one's external and internal selves to be inseparably interlinked. It is relevant to note that Qazis and Muftis also agree with the fact that one's external and internal selves should be inseparably interlinked, without any trace of contradictions between the two. By virtue of these things, *Treeqat* and *Shariat* are complementary to each other. Summarily speaking, they are inseparable.

Question: If Allah is Omnipresent, why do the Muslims living in the east face the west while praying Salah?

Answer: No doubt, Allah is present everywhere. Our facing Kaba while in the state of prayer is a symbolic affirmation of our belief that Allah is Omnipresent. It is not that the Muslims living in the east face the west. The Muslims living anywhere in the world face while in the state of their five daily prayers, as also other prayers. In this way the votaries of prayer in the world make a circle around the Kaba to bow down before Allah and sing only His glory in their prayers.

Question: Normally the Muslims wear different types of dresses like pants and shirts, kurta and pyjama, etc. Does Islam have some strict dress code for its followers?

Answer: Islam has no strict dress code. But it does ensure that people wear clothes to cover the concealable parts of their bodies. It stresses that people wear such clothes in which they can sit and revert to standing position and walk comfortably. Needless to mention, that Islam believes that clothes should not be the symbol of pride and arrogance.

Question: The Muslims recite some verses of the Qur'an with some eatables in front of them. They term it as Fateha. They distribute the eatables among the poor. Why don't they give a pretty good part of their earning in charity to poor Muslims? If they do so, there will remain no poor Muslim.

Answer: The Muslims dispense charity and feed the poor. At the same time, they also give Zakat (alms) and charity in order to help the poor. The teaching of Islam encourages them for charity and dispensing financial assistance to the needy. Allah promises them to reward them beyond measures.

Question: If a Muslim does not strictly observe some Islamic laws for a brief period of time with an intention to promote communal harmony, will his belief be questioned?

Answer: Communal harmony achieved through such means does not deserve to be rightly called communal harmony. The act of abandoning one's religious belief is indicative of internal feud and dissension. It bears witness to the fact that the intended harmony is not achieved. Communal harmony exists in our fortitude, patience, tolerance and reverence of other religions. True religious spirit inculcates in us the virtues of accepting others with their individual qualities and beliefs. I believe every religion teaches co-existence.

Question: Does Islam permit the believers to live like a recluse?

Answer: Islam does not allow Muslims to live like a recluse. It urges the people to live in society with social duties, obligations and rights.

Question: Does Islam permit the believers to wreak vengeance on others?

Answer: As evidenced by the Qur'an, Allah delivers justice. He loves justice and the just. Prophet Muhammad (Pbuh) never preferred to take revenge on others. Similarly, Allah loves those who forgive and seek forgiveness. One can easily trace the most ideal examples of granting forgiveness in the life of Prophet Muhammad (Pbuh), as also one can learn a lot from his conduct with the war captives of the battle of Badr. His noble conduct with the people of Makkah after his conquest over Makkah is yet another glowing example of forgiveness and co-existence. While on the other hand, the people of Makkah had subjected Prophet Muhammad (Pbuh) and his companions to ruthless cruelties. Even then Prophet Muhammad (Pbuh) forgave them. Moreover, he forgave even the killer of his beloved uncle Hazrat Hamza. Revenge is a negative impulse. It has no place in the canons of Islam.

Question: Zakat is obligatory. Should those who give Zakat consult their elders or should they give it without any consultation with them?

Answer: One who pays Zakat can give it to any deserving recipient he likes. If he is a member of an extended family and the sum of Zakat is pooled, he can dispense his Zakat in consultation with his elders.

Question: Suppose a boy and a girl establish illicit relations. Now they want to enter into marriage with each other, will marriage be treated valid?

Answer: They can enter into marriage but the sin committed by them cannot be forgiven. As per the Islamic laws, they will be meted out to severe punishment.

Question: If a girl and a boy commit adultery by fault and later on they come to know about their mistake. Then they undergo a true repentance, will Allah forgive them? If they do not commit any sins afterwards, will they be forgiven by Allah and admitted to heaven? If the boy happens to meet her and remembers his mistake, how he will feel? Suppose they are admitted to heaven, will they recognise each other?

Answer: Adultery may be committed by fault only in case when two brides married at the same time are exchanged by mistake. It is known as '*subhatul watee*'. As regards repentance, Allah forgives those who repent sincerely. He is all merciful and kind. He knows the best as to who will be admitted to heaven and who will be thrust into hell. According to my understanding of the Hadith and Qur'an, heaven is a place of blissful happiness beyond measures and repentance will not come near people in heaven.

Question: Most of the votaries of Juma prayer offer only two obligatory cycles of prayer. They go out without performing Sunnah and voluntary cycles of prayer. Will Allah accept their prayers?

Answer: If a votary of prayer performs only two obligatory cycles of prayer and leaves the mosque for his home, he performs Sunnah and other cycles of prayers at his home. It is in full consonance with the Islamic injunction to perform Sunnah and other cycles of prayer at one's home. Prophet Muhammad (Pbuh) is reported to have said, "Turn not your homes into a graveyard". It means that votaries of prayer should perform Sunnah and Nafl prayers at their homes.

Question: Why do the Muslims hold Thursday as a good day for dispensing charity?

Answer: Thursday is treated as the weekend by the Muslims. As regards Friday, it is also an important day for the Muslims because Prophet Muhammad (Pbuh) used to gather people in the Mosque of the Madinah during the night between Thursday and Friday. Friday is also called a smaller Eid. Needless to say, the Muslims have been commanded to dispense charity among the poor before the celebration of Eid. It is evidently clear that the practice of dispensing charity on Thursday is in conformity with this tradition. It is also pertinent to mention here that there is no fixed day for dispensing charity. One should dispense it as and when one gets the opportunity.

Question: Suppose a Muslim adopts the practices of some other religion or he turns an apostate, but he wants to enter the fold of Islam once again, will he be allowed to embrace the faith of Islam?

Answer: If a Muslim turns an apostate and then repents sincerely and brings himself to accept Islam again, he will find that Allah forgives him. The true expiation of his sinfulness consists in his sincere attempt of seeking Allah's forgiveness and bringing himself to true repentance with undivided loyalty to Allah.

Question: If a non-Muslim embraces Islam, will he be required to undergo circumcision?

Answer: According to Hanafi school of thought it is a desirable tradition, whereas it is compulsory according to Shafaee and Maliki schools of thought.

Question: If a female is not in the permissible state of reading the Qur'an, but, she happens to read it. Then she repents sincerely, will she be forgiven? What is she supposed to do?

Answer: If she does it by fault, she is not held liable for a punishment. But one is required to repent sincerely for such mistakes.

Question: If a goat kept for sacrifice, breaks its horn, leg, or has its ears cut or is blinded, it is not fit to be slaughtered as a sacrificial animal. On the contrary, a he-goat is castrated, making him deprived of one part of body. Sometimes it is paralysed. It also causes a deformity. How can this he-goat be fit for sacrifice?

Answer: Of course, it is not allowed to slaughter an animal with a physical deformity. But castration is done not for causing a physical deformity to the he-goat. It also does no harm the animal. But its meat becomes tasty by virtue of castration.

Question: Some Muslims avoid using the milk of jersey cows. They believe that they born after a cow is crossbred by semen of a pig. If it is true, can Islam permit one to use the milk of these cows?

Answer: I have no knowledge about it from the reliable sources. But it goes without saying that the Muslims are strictly forbidden to use pig's hair, skin, flesh, blood, semen and so on.

Question: Can a Muslim be polytheist? If it is so, how can it be possible?

Answer: Muslims can never be polytheists. Islam and polytheisms are diametrically opposed to each other.

Question: There is a tradition called circumcision among the Muslims as well as among the Jews. What are the practical and scientific merits of this practice?

Answer: Circumcision is a tradition of Hazarat Ibraheem (a.s.). It is practised by the Jews and Muslims. It protects males from different types of diseases.

Question: Please tell me the prayer which does not need to be repeated after it has been invalidated due to certain causes.

Answer: If the votaries of Eid prayer come to know, after reaching their homes, that they had made some mistakes during their prayer, it is not necessary for them to repeat that prayer. Similarly, if the votaries of Juma prayer come to know about the mistakes, they made during the prayer after the time for Juma has expired, it is not necessary for them to repeat Juma prayer.

Question: If a votary of prayer ties some piece of cloth on his head with an intention to cover or in consonance with some existing fashion, or under some compulsion, will such prayer be valid?

Answer: The most important thing in prayer is that the forehead and nose must touch the earth. The purpose here is to purge the votaries of prayer of pride and arrogance. If a votary of prayer prays with forehead covered, his prayer will be valid. But one could better perform with an uncovered forehead.

Question: Name the impurity which can be removed without water.

Answer: There are many situations when one can obtain cleanliness without water. For example, one can use a dry piece of soil for obtaining cleanliness after one's natural call. If there is some impure matter lying on a patch of land and it dries itself, no water is needed for obtaining the purity from that patch of land.

Question: There was a King named Zulqarnain. Name the prophet of Allah after whom he came to rule. If it was after Christ, name the period.

Answer: As mentioned by Maulana Abul Kalam Azad in his interpretation of the Qur'an, there was a King namely Cyrus before 560 BC. He is also called Zulqarnain. It is evidently clear that he ruled before Hazarat Isa (a.s.).

Question: Is it lawful to believe in Astronomy? If yes, is it an act of infidelity? People say that one reaps the reward of one's deeds. On the other hand, our religion says that nothing happens without the will of Allah, whereas the astronomers say that everything depends on the constellation of stars. I am in a fix as to what I should accept and what I should reject?

Answer: Islam lays emphasis on the belief that every human being reaps as he sows. The result, good or bad is predestined by Allah. We seek the remedy for the diseases in medicines and other things with medicinal properties with complete reliance on Allah and His kindness. So, one should try one's best to stay loyal Allah, under all circumstances with constant perseverance and complete reliance on Him only.

Question: Barailawis say that one should stand up in the gathering of Milad for invoking Allah's blessing and sending Salam on to Prophet

Muhammad (Pbuh). They say that the Prophet (Pbuh) comes there in person. What do you think?

Answer: Differences of opinions regarding sending Salam onto Prophet (Pbuh) in standing position, trace the origin in individual interpretations. I think we should respect others' emotions and sentiments.

Question: What type of education is prescribed by Islam? Is it permissible for one true Muslim to acquire secular education?

Answer: Islam does not demarcate between religious and secular educations because education can have no watertight compartmentalisation on the basis of religion. The first word of the Qur'an revealed to Prophet Muhammad (Pbuh) was 'Iqra' which literally means 'read'. This Surah testifies the importance of education and pen. Allah declares Hadrat Adam to be superior to the angles because the former knew what the latter did not know. Hadrat Adam was taught by Allah. Prophet Muhammad (Pbuh) encouraged the people to acquire knowledge. He stressed that this noble act should be carried from cradle to the grave. He is also reported to have said, "It is obligatory on every Muslim male and female to attain education". In sum, he did not distinguish between religious knowledge and secular education. One can easily trace its practical examples in his life. After the battle of Badr, he released Jew war captives on the condition that they would teach Muslim boys and girls in Madinah. Then they would be allowed to go back to Makkah. Needless to say, the Prophet (Pbuh) did not ask the Jews, sworn enemies of Islam, to impart religious education. Evidently enough, the Muslims are lawfully permitted to receive religious as well as secular education. But they should wisely avoid the knowledge that is against the welfare of humanity and the universe.

Question: Does Islam permit the female votaries of prayer to pray in Mosques?

Answer: Yes, it does. The books on Islamic jurisprudence record the instructions of praying congregational prayer in mosques. But in view of evils prevailing in the society, people decided by a general consensus that it would only be proper for women to perform their five daily prayers inside their houses, if there is no separate arrangement for them in mosques. Evidently, it is not essential for women to perform five daily prayers in congregation like males votaries of prayers.

Question: Please tell us special virtues of Asr and Fajr prayers. What is the importance of the figures 786 and 92?

Answer: Every obligatory cycle of five daily prayer – be it Fajr, Zuhr and so on, has the same importance and rewards. The figure 786 stand for Bismillah-hir-Rahman-ir-Rahim. Similarly, the figure 92 stand for Muhammad (Pbuh). People use these figures in order to safeguard the Bismillah-hir-Rahman-ir-Rahim and Muhammad against disrespect in any form.

Question: Can a Muslim seek help from anyone else other than Allah? Can he be of some avail to someone like Allah?

Answer: According to Islamic belief, every Muslim has to worship Allah alone and seek help from none but Him. There is no denying of the fact that none but Allah has the power to avail others and solve their problems. We should not call anyone else against Allah for help. No help can come to us, if Allah does not want to help us.

Question: Suppose one is fasting. Now if one stays in the state of uncleanliness for first half of the day and stays in the state of cleanliness for the other half of the day, will his fast be valid?

Answer: His fast will be valid. But one should not stay in the state of uncleanliness.

Question: If we slaughter sacrificial animals on behalf of our deceased relatives, will the sacrifices fetch rewards to them?

Answer: It is permissible for one to slaughter a sacrificial animal in behalf of a dead person. But first of all, it is compulsory for him to slaughter a sacrificial animal obligatory on him. If he has sufficient resources, he can slaughter a sacrificial animal in behalf of his deceased relative. As regard the rewards, Allah attaches importance to the intention. He is very kind and merciful.

Question: In other countries, the mosques do not have any worship houses of other religions beside them. But in India several mosques are there beside temples in cities like Ayodhya, Mathura and Benaras. If Islam promotes coexistence of people of different religions, why don't the Muslim brothers let their mosques be shifted to other places?

Answer: India is a country of ethnic, cultural, lingual and religious diversity in the strict sense of the word. This country has been blessed with every season. Eighteen languages are recognised by the Constitution and enjoy equal status. India presents a true example and an ideal model of unity in diversity. Our worshipping houses built side by side bear testimony to our mutual coexistence, love, brotherhood, amity and peace. We accord reverence to the religious rituals of every religion. If we look at other countries, we will lose our identity. We should feel proud of our ideal unity.

Question: I know some people belonging to the sect, called Ahl-e-Sunnat, who display pictures of Dul Dul and Burraq. While on the other hand, people of Deoband and Ahl-e-Hdith Schools of thought do not approve of possessing or hanging such pictures. What is your opinion?

Answer: In Islam, there is no evidence of any instructions for hanging the pictures of Dul Dul and Burraq. Even Ala Hazrat Fazil Barailawi is against such things.

Question: There is a tomb right in front of one mosque. There are some people who go straight to the tomb and perform their prayer over there. They do not go to mosque for the prayer. Is it permissible for one to do so?

Answer: One should pray in mosques.

Question: Quite frequently, I have seen people changing their places in the mosques to perform their prayers. For instance, one performs one's obligatory cycles of prayer at one place in the mosque but he shifts to another place for praying Sunnah cycles of prayers. Is one not allowed to perform Sunnah cycle of prayer at the same spot where one prays obligatory cycles of prayer?

Answer: It is not prohibited for one to perform Sunnah cycles of prayer at the same place where one performs obligatory cycles of prayer. One shifts from one place to another, so that one can prostrate at different places on the earth. After the performance of the obligatory cycles of prayer in mosque, one can also pray Sunnah and Nafl prayers at one's house.

Question: Islam prohibits one from clicking a picture. Can one's voice be recorded? Can it be heard after one dies?

Answer: One can record one's voice and others can listen to it after one dies.

Question: The knowledge about any aspect of Islam traces its origin in the Qur'an and life of the Prophet Muhammad (Pbuh), only. What is your opinion?

Answer: I agree with you.

Question: According to the explanation of the scholars of Islam, the words of the Islamic 'kalima' mean "None but Allah is worthy of worship and

Prophet Muhammad (Pbuh) is the messenger of Allah". Kindly quote the exact words of 'kalima' and tell the exact translation of every word.

Answer: 'La ilaha illallah' means "No one is worthy of worship except Allah". And the expression 'Muhammad-ur-Rasulallah' means "Muhammad (Pbuh) is the messenger of Allah". The word 'rasool' means sent down. 'La' means no, 'ilah' means, 'worthy of worship', 'ila' means but. The thrust of the 'kalima' is that human beings should not bow down before anyone else other than Allah.

Question: I am a neo-Muslim. I have been teaching some children the Qur'an for some time now. I learnt how to read the Qur'an after my marriage. I pronounce 'alif zer' 'e'. But someone told me that it is 'alif zer' 'ee'. Which one is correct?

Answer: Allah rewards one for one's intention and deeds. Closer to us than our jugular veins, He knows our innermost desires. You should continue your good deed – the act of teaching the Qur'an. As regards the pronunciation, it is 'alif zer' 'ee'.

Question: Allah sent down numerous messengers. Many of them find mention in heavenly Books, the Qur'an, the Bible and the Taurat. Their names are almost the same in every heavenly Book. What is then the difference between the Bible and the Qur'an? So, there should not be any differences of opinion regarding religion of Jews, Muslims and Christians.

Answer: According to Islamic belief, the Creator of this universe is Allah. All human beings are the children of Adam and Hawwa (a.s.). Allah sent down prophets to every community that existed in the world. The names of some communities are known to us. Hazrat Musa (a.s.) and Hazrat Isa (a.s.) were the true messengers of Allah. Allah revealed to them Taurat and Injeel. It is important to mention here that every Muslim is required to believe in these Prophets and in the Books revealed to them by Allah. According to Islamic belief, the Jews and Christians did not follow the messages of Allah as taught to them by their Prophets in true spirit. The Qur'an bears witness to it. This is the main reason of differences among them.

Question: Suppose there is a votary of five daily prayers who also listens to the news and songs broadcast by the radio. What are the Islamic injunctions about such a person?

Answer: Performance of five daily prayers is an obligatory duty of every Muslim. There is no harm in listening to the news bulletin. Needless to say, one must wisely avoid vulgar and obscene things.

Question: Did Islam, especially during the revelation of the Qur'an and jotting down of Hadith, allow sterilisation? T. V. and cinema were not there those days, why do the scholars of Islam prohibit the Muslims from watching them? Aren't they impeding the development of the Muslims and making Islam a backward religion?

Answer: As recorded in some books on Islamic history sterilisation existed during the lifetime of the Prophet (Pbuh). Though Islam does not oppose sterilisation, it is incumbent on one to abide by the man-made rules like that of sterilisation. It is so because it may be harmful for human beings as well as the society. Islam does not oppose the means of communication like TV and cinema. It is dead against those programmes which not only cause moral and social decline but also encourage immorality and depravity.

Question: Should one who is going to undertake the journey to Makkah for paying the pilgrimage to the holy house of Allah meet his enemies and sink his differences with them? If his mother does not forgive him before he sets out for the journey to Makkah, will Allah accept his Hajj?

Answer: Islam teaches us to avoid perpetrating any sort of cruelties on any one. Further, if one has hurt anyone, he or she should sink differences by seeking his or her forgiveness. Allah does not forgive one unless a person who has been affected forgives. If a pilgrim pays attention to these things, it is very good. As regards the acceptance of Hajj by Allah, it is upto Him to accept or reject it. If one's mother is angry due to anything genuine, one will earn Allah's wrath. There goes a Hadith which means that if one earns the pleasure of one's parents, one earns the pleasure of Allah and if one earns the displeasure of one's parents, one incurs the displeasure of Allah. If he repents for his mistakes sincerely, Allah forgives him. But he is required to be first be forgiven by his parents. It is but a human nature to commit mistakes. At the same time, the act of forgiveness earns one Allah's pleasure.

Question: Shia and Sunni are the names of two Muslim sects. Are there any differences in the ways of their performance of five daily Salah? What is the meaning of Salah?

Answer: Salah means to pray. While in the state of prayer, the slave of Allah prays to Him with all due humility and total loyalty to Him. So, be one a Shia or Sunni, one prays to Allah with humility and total loyalty to Him. Fundamentally, five daily prayers of Shia and Sunni are the same. They may differ from each other only in some ways of performing them.

Question: Will the act of waging war with swords and modern weapons against polytheism and against those who perpetrate cruelties on the weak be called Jihad? There goes a Hadith which means that heaven lies under the shadows of swords. What is your opinion?

Answer: Only a model Islamic state has the right to wage Jihad. Indeed Jihad is never waged for power, wealth, personal glory or national fervour. It is fought with the objective of establishing and defending the rights of civil and religious liberty, repelling and preventing the hostilities and persecution. It is also for the establishment of peaceful atmosphere in society. On the other hand, Islam motivates us to counter the oppressors with patience and perseverance. Allah takes the oath by time and says in the Qur'an that those who believe and do good deeds steadfastly and persevere patiently and thoughtfully, will be among the successful people. History bears witness to the fact that violence and hatred breed worst form of violence and hatred. On the contrary, non-violence, kindness and positive attitude pave the way for love and affection, fraternity and brotherhood, and amity and peace.

Question: A scholar of Islam of our neighbouring country says that India is Darul Harb. So, the Indian Muslims can take bank interest. What is your opinion?

Answer: India is not a Darul Harb. It is Darussulah. Since it is not a Darul Harb, any argument in favour of taking bank interest is meaningless.

Question: Is usury forbidden for Muslims? Is renting out one's house to a tenant also forbidden? I think both usury and renting out one's house fetch money to one without one's putting any physical labour. What is your opinion?

Answer: Both giving and taking usury are strictly forbidden in Islam. This practice creates an imbalance in society. If the rich give money to the people belonging to the working class on usurious interest, a big chunk of the earnings of poor workers will go to the rich usurers. And they will be trapped in a vicious circle. The usurer earns money without any physical or mental labour. As regards renting out a house, it is entirely different. One invests money to build a house and then earns money by renting it out. It is a kind of business. So, it is permissible to rent out one's house.

Question: There is a Muslim. He is a cheat, fraud and evil doer. But he also performs five daily prayers regularly and dispenses charity. What is your opinion about him? Allah is kind and merciful. Will He forgive such a Muslim in return of his performance of Salah and dispensing charity? If

Allah can forgive such a person, why should a non-believer believe in Him?

Answer: Islam primarily promotes peace and amity among people. It aims at rooting out all evils prevalent in the society. One's performance of prayer and dispensing charity will not earn Allah's forgiveness for the evils acts one does. Salah and fasting are called the rights of Allah. Allah can forgive one for one's shortcomings while praying or fasting. But the social evil deeds have adverse effects on human beings. Allah will not forgive him unless the persons who have been harmed forgive him. Needless to say, prayer, fasting and other acts of worship prohibit one from indulging in evil acts. If one does not mend one's bad habits, one has to pray with more sincerity and undivided loyalty to Allah. Allah may accept everyone's acts of worship.

Question: What are the Islamic injunctions regarding the donation and replacements of organs and also blood donation?

Answer: It is lawful to donate and receive blood for the sake of saving a human life. As regards the donation or replacement of some body organs, a meeting of Rabta-e-Islami Fiqh Academy held in Makkah Mukarramah on 28th Rabius-Sani, 1405 Hijri. It was decided that people could receive or donate body organs in their life-time. The organs could be donated even after death. The decisions taken are as follows: 1. The donation of the organs of body should neither be life-threatening nor should involve complications in later stage of one's life. The principle of Islamic Sharia prevents such acts that involve risk for others. 2. The donor of the organ should donate it willingly without succumbing to any pressure or greed. 3. Replacement of the organs must be the only option left for the patient. 4. One has to ensure that replacement of the body organs is feasible and would be successful. The following conditions are applicable in case a body organ of a dead person is donated: 1. The body organs of the dead person can be donated on the condition that he had given the permission in his life-time. 2. If there be a need, the patient can receive the body organs of healthy and slaughtered animals. 3. It is allowed to take one's healthy part of skin or flesh to graft at other place of the same person. Similarly, his bone of one place may be fixed at any other place. It is also allowed to use an artificial metallic thing for replacing the bones or heart valve. These are four states which are lawful with suitable conditions. (Ref: Fiqhi Faisle: Asre Hazir ke Pecheda Masail ke Bare mein, Rabta Aalam-e-Islami, Islamic Fiqh Academy, Makkah Mukarramah ke Aham Fiqhi Faisle, Quazi Mujahi-dul-Islam

Qasmi, Urdu translation by Muhammad Faheem Akhtar Nadvi, Islamic Fiqh Academy, pp 157-158).

Question: My father invites his non-Muslim friends on the occasion of Eid-ul Azha. He serves them with sacrificial meat and wine. What kind of punishment will be meted out to him?

Answer: It is a major sin to drink and serve wine to others. In Islamic states, a drunker is lashed with whips in public. The act of slaughtering a sacrificial animal symbolises one's willingness and readiness to lay down one's life for the Creator and for holding the Truth aloft. Now, if someone serves one's guests with the meat of a sacrificial animal and wine, one is a proven guilty of a major sin. It is quite unfortunate that your father is treating Islamic Sharia sacrilegiously in place of staying obedient and respectful to Allah and His commands. He is ruining his probationary life on this earth as also the life hereafter. May Allah show him the right path and make him be from among those who walk in the light of His grace!

Question: Is a fresh Aqiqa required for renaming the child? If a he-goat was sacrificed for the first Aqiqa, can one slaughter a big animal for the second one?

Answer: No second Aqiqa is required for renaming a child.

Question: The Qur'an commands, "Establish prayer". Aren't the acts of establishing prayer and performing it the same?

Answer: The meaning of "Establishing prayer" is performing prayer as well as inviting others to pray. It also implies the creations of an atmosphere conducive to the performance of prayer for everybody.

Question: What is the logic behind performing five daily prayers?

Answer: Allah commanded His slaves to do those acts which are beneficial to human life. We have been created with a serious purpose. It demands us to be worshipful and obedient to our Lord in every sphere of life. We should be mindful of the serious purpose behind our creation and have to bring ourselves to the devotional piety with full obeisance and servitude to Allah. There are individual as well as collective merits of the performance of prayer. The individual merits are: reminding one of the serious purpose of one's creation, creating-duty consciousness, character-building, endowing one with power of conquest over one's lower 'self' and so on. The collective merits include: coaching people into discipline, inculcating in them the quality to follow true leaders, fostering the sense of equality, brotherhood, creating love for straightforwardness, punctuality, humility and so on.

Question: The Islamic caliphate started in Madinah. Did politics also start there? To the Arabs politics means ruling over the people. Caliphate is also a type of ruling over the people. What is your opinion?

Answer: The Islamic caliphate cannot be compared with contemporary world politics. In a caliphate Allah and His laws are above all. Everything is governed in the light of His laws. And every human being enjoys equal status there.

Question: What is the meaning of Zulqarnain?

Answer: The question has already been answered in this book, elsewhere, with another angle. Here is an answer again. As recorded in Farhang-e-Asiafiya, an Urdu Lexicon, Zulqarnain means one who has two horns or two tufts or strands of hair. Sikandar, the great had this feature. People believe that he was named Zulqarnain either because of the two strands of hair or two horns. According to other interpretation Zulqarnain mentioned in the Qur'an is not Sikandar, the great. It was some other King because there is a long gap between the periods of these two kings. The reason of keeping Zulqarnain as the name was that Sikandar, the great, had fixed two horns on his throne after his conquest over Iran. The horns of a goat and a he-goat refer to the throne of Greece and horns of a sheep refer to the throne of Iran. After the conquest over Iran, all Iranian and Jews had become his subjects. According to the historians, he died in 323 BC or in 332 BC in Babul at the age of 32 or 33.

Question: Is it permissible to read to the Qur'an in Hindi version? Do the copies of the Qur'an in Hindi and Arabic versions have the same importance? If one reads Hindi version of the Qur'an; will he earn the same rewards?

Answer: It is permissible for one to recite the Qur'an in Hindi version. One should recite verses from the Hindi version, if one is not able to recite them in Arabic. But one must try one's best to learn how to recite them according to Arabic phonetic line. Allah rewards one profusely for one's worshipful acts.

Question: Are the people of every Islamic set regarded as Muslims?

Answer: Those who believe in the Qur'an, Hadith and act according to them, are the believers. Of course, there are certain differences of opinion among them regarding certain matters. And the root of the differences of opinion lies in interpretations of some verses of the Qur'an and some Ahadith. As far as basic articles of faith are concerned, there is no difference of opinion among them.

Question: Suppose someone has money to be dispensed in charity. Is it lawful for one to change one's one five hundred rupee note for five hundred rupee notes from the money kept separately for charity?
Answer: It is permissible. But one should take as much money as one gives.

Question: Some Indian spiritual, religious and social leaders broke with many traditional practices so that they could reform the society. For example, Mahavir offered sacrificial animal in wars, Swami Dayanand worshipped idols and Mahatma Gandhi raised his voice against untouchability. Have some Islamic leaders been regarded as great leaders by virtue of raising their voice against wrong social practices.
Answer: Basic articles of faith, principles and values of Islamic codes have always been the same. There is no debate among the Muslims over them. Several scholars of Islam and Muslim Sufis launched movements and carried out their campaigns for the dissemination of the Islamic teachings of equality, sympathy, love and affection, patience and perseverance, true spirit of philanthropy and oneness of Allah. Thus, they inculcated true values of Islam in people. One can appropriately mention in this respect, the names of Khwaja Moinuddin Chishti, Hazrat Nizamuddin Auliya, Hazrat Shaikh Ahmad Sarhindi, Shah Waliullah, Sir Syed Ahmad Khan, Allama Iqbal, Maulana Ashraf Ali Thanvi, Maulana Abul Kalam Azad, Abul Ala Maududi and so on.

Question: When did Prophet Muhammad (Pbuh) start praying Salah?
Answer: Every messenger and Prophet of Allah worshipped Allah according to His guidance. Five daily prayers were made obligatory during the Prophet's (Pbuh) celestial ascension (me'raj).

Question: Is it lawful to make Tazia and recite some verses of the Qur'an with Tazia for the sake of a practice called Fateha. Can this practice be substantiated with some prophetic traditions (Hadith)?
Answer: One cannot substantiate this practice with Hadith.

Question: Is it permissible for the Muslim males to apply henna (mehndi)?
Answer: It is in consonance with the prophetic tradition to apply henna on one's head and beard. But they are not allowed to put henna on their hands and feet. Only women are allowed to put henna on their hands and

feet for the sake of ornamentation. Obviously, males should wisely avoid it. But one is permitted to use it as a medicine, in case there is a need.

Question: Suppose there is a Muslim male. He does not have the requisite knowledge of Islam. Should he go with the people of Tableeghi Jamaat for learning Islam or should he first shoulder his household responsibilities? The people involved in Tableeghi Jamaat say, if one leaves one's home for the sake of Allah, Allah sets everything right.

Answer: Everyone has primarily two responsibilities: 1. Responsibilities towards himself, the members of his family and society. 2. Responsibilities towards Allah. No doubt, Allah is the most kind and merciful. If one is deficient in His worship, Allah may forgive one. But He will not forgive one for one's neglectful attitude towards one's family members. He will not forgive one until one has been forgiven by members of the family. Of course, it is obligatory to attain knowledge of Islam and its rulings but preference should be give to one's family and the society.

Question: Are only Muslims permitted to enter Madinah Munawwarah and Makkah Mukarramah?

Answer: Yes, none but Muslims are allowed to enter Madinah Munawwarah and Makkah Mukarramah.

Question: Some Muslims go to different mausoleums of saints and bow down before their graves. Islam does not allow anyone to bow down before anyone other than Allah. What is your opinion?

Answer: The scholars of Islam of every school of thought forbid the act of bowing down in front of a grave. But some people following the Sufi tradition believe that it is lawful to pay the prostration of respect. One can refer to Khwaja Hasan Nizami's Book "Sajda-e-Tazeemi", prostration of respect. He distinguishes Sajda-e-Tazeemi from Sajda-e-Ta'budi, devotional prostration paid to none but Allah.

Question: Is it permissible for a Muslim to hold a marriage ceremony during the month of Moharram?

Answer: Islam does not prohibit one from celebrating the marriage during the month of Moharram. Since during this month, the most tragic event – martyrdom of Hazrat Imam Husain and his companions took place, the Muslims appropriately avoid holding marriage ceremonies during this month.

Question: If there is a Muslim who does not pray and says that he is irreligious; can he still remain a Muslim?

Answer: If one publicly says that one is irreligious, it is an idle thing to see whether one remains a Muslim or not.

Question: In most of Hindi films, a terrorist is found necessarily to be a Muslim. I think this act of Indian film industry has led the Hindus nurse a feeling of hatred against the Muslims. Censor Board should not pass such films. What is your opinion?

Answer: I think it is not correct. Good and bad characters are taken from every religion and community. Our film industry has been away from religious biases.

Question: If Islam does not allow untouchability, why don't the Muslims allow the people of other religions to enter their worship houses?

Answer: Islam teaches us the true concept of equality, love and brotherhood. It never allows its people to divide the world on the basis of caste, race, and language. It also imparts the lesson that all human beings constitute the family of Allah, and Allah loves those who love His family the most. Further, it is integral to our belief that Allah is the Creator of the universe and all human beings are the offsprings of Adam and Hawwa (a.s.). In his address delivered on the occasion of the last Hajj, Prophet Muhammad (Pbuh) said, "The best among the people is one who is the best in conduct, piety and good deeds, and also the most Allah fearing."

Question: Why are the Muslim women so backward? Isn't it ironical that both the purdah (veil) system and divorce exist in the Muslim society? Why do the scholars of Islam discourage women education?

Answer: Certainly, the Muslim women are quite backward. But we should keep it in mind that their condition can't be bettered in the absence of good economic and educational conditions they are far behind the Muslim males. The Muslims have been educationally backward for last 72 years. One can verify it by the data collected by the Government agencies. Veil and divorce are no impediments for the Muslim women to grow.

Question: It is not permissible for one to hang pictures on the walls of one's house. How can then watching TV be lawful? Islam can't allow dancing and singing. Is it so that they are lawful according to Brailawis and unlawful according to Deobandis?

Answer: The question related to the photographs has already been answered. It has nothing to do with the scholars of various schools of thought. It is permissible for one to watch informative, educational, social, religious and political TV programmes. But there is no compulsion for one to watch these TV programmes. One may or may not like to watch them. The scholars of Islam unanimously agree that one can watch such programmes. But Islam never allows nudity, vulgarity and obscenity in any form.

Question: If someone buys a he-goat for Rs. 1800. Unfortunately, it dies before the celebration of Eid-ul Azha. Is it necessary for one to buy a he-goat for Rs. 1800? If one doesn't do it, will one be liable to punishment?

Answer: According to Hanafi jurisprudence one who possesses so much wealth that he is liable to pay Alms, then he should slaughter a sacrificial animal in the name of Allah on the occasion of Eid-ul Azha. If one's goat dies, one has to buy another one. But it is not necessary for one to buy another goat for the same amount. But according to the Ahl-e-Hadith school of thought, it is not necessary for one to slaughter another animal, if one does not have the necessary means. It is so because he had earlier bought the animal with full intention to slaughter it as a sacrificial animal in the name of Allah.

Question: If someone keeps the money for dispensing Zakat in his pocket and unfortunately his pocket is picked up; will his Zakat be treated as paid? Or, should he arrange money and dispense Zakat?

Answer: According to Hanafi jurisprudence, one has to arrange money to pay Zakat because the amount of Zakat due on him has not been paid by him as Zakat. But according to Ahl-e-Hadith school of thought, it will be deemed to have been paid because he had already separated the amount of Zakat due on him. So, he will not be required to pay it again.

Question: Do some votaries of prayer perform their prayers in Masjid-al-Aqsa? Is it really under the custody of the Jews?

Answer: Yes, some votaries of prayer pray in Masjid-al-Aqsa. It is under the custody of the Jews.

Question: Some Muslims believe that one's act of driving a pig away with a cane or with a stone leaves one in a state of uncleanliness. They say that such a person has to take a bath. Isn't such belief a mark of the Muslims' being quite backward in thoughts? I think such trifle and petty issues and traditions stunt the mental and physical growth of people. What is your opinion?

Answer: Those who are not familiar with the spirit of Islam properly, get enmeshed in such petty issues. Islam is a perfect and ideal way of life. Those who embrace it and follow its teaching with full obedience to Allah prosper and grow mentally as well as physically. Of course, the system prescribed by Islam does harmonise nature and fulfills the demands of the society.

Question: Has Allah created something better than human beings? Is Allah on Arsh? Isn't it strange that He is on Arsh and His abode is on the earth?

Answer: This question is basically concerned with belief. One can't always reach the truth with help of analogical deductions. According to the Islam, human beings are Allah's best creation. Allah is on Arsh but nothing in the universe is beyond His control. One can remember Allah anywhere in the universe. The entire earth has been described as a place of prostration. A Mosque, which is called a House of Allah, is a place of Allah's worship. But it can't be used for any worldly purposes.

Question: There are some people who extract money from others in the name of giving amulets and so, called exorcising evil spirit and so on. They use such money for meeting the expense of their journey to Makkah for paying pilgrimage to the holy house of Allah and also for building Madrasas. What is your opinion about it?

Answer: According to the Islamic belief, both one's means and earnings should be lawful. It is not permissible for one to opt for amulet making and exorcising as a profession.

Question: Sometimes people bring soil from some other place to repair the graves. They wish the graves to be identified as graves from some distance as well. Is it permissible?

Answer: Prophet Muhammad (Pbuh) forbade us to plaster the graves with cement. But it is permissible to bring the soil from other places to repair a grave.

Question: I am a teacher, I embraced Islam six years ago. The members of my family, including my wife and children, are angry with me. They are pressurising me to revert to my old religion. What should I do?

Answer: If you have embraced Islam after a mature thought and in consonance with your inner voice, it is up to you to explore the ways through which you can develop a perfect harmony with the members of your family.

Question: What is Tableeghi Jamaat? Is it permissible for ten or fifteen people to go to a mosque and stay there for several days and nights?

Answer: It was started in 1934 by Maulana Muhammad Ilyas, with the objectives to preach Islam, make the Muslims punctual to five daily prayers, fasting and other acts of worship that they owe to Allah. They ask the people to assemble at a certain place, chalk out their daily programmes to teach those Muslims who do not know how to make ablution, how to pray and how to recite the Qur'an. People associated with this Jamaat, do not want to stay at someone's place, so they stay in mosques.

Question: The Imams leading Maghrib, Isha and Fajr prayers recite the Qur'an audibly. Why don't they recite the Qur'an audibly in Zuhr and Asr prayers?

Answer: Five daily prayers are performed in the way they were performed by Prophet Muhammad (Pbuh). Moreover, it seems that the Imams don't recite the Qur'an audibly while performing Zuhr and Asr because there is already a lot of hustle and bustle in the localities.

Question: Some people invoke Allah's blessings and send Salam on to the Prophet (Pbuh) audibly in their standing position in front of the holy grave of the Prophet in Madinah. The scholars of Deobandi school of thought object to it. What is the problem in audible invocation of Allah's blessings and sending Salam to the Prophet (Pbuh)?

Answer: We should have no objection to the invocation of Allah's blessings on to Prophet (Pbuh) in standing position with one's hands placed near one's naval point. But our tone should be gentle. The Qur'an commanded the companions of the Prophet (Pbuh) not to raise their voice above the voice of the Prophet. So, we should be mindful of Allah command. One may read *Suratul Hujurat,* for more information in this respect.

Question: Some people are of the opinion that the number of women thrust into hell will outnumber the males. Strictly speaking, Muslim males also commit sinful acts. But their misdeeds are ignored now-a-days. What is your opinion?

Answer: It is up to Allah to decide as to who will be admitted to heaven and who will be thrust into hell. Allah makes no distinction between males and females. He determines the rewards and punishment on the basis of good and bad deeds. He will never punish one person for some else's mistakes. The best in His sight is one who is the most righteous and dutiful in obeying the commands of Allah.

Question: Why are Qadyanis treated to be out of the fold of Islam? Did Mirza Ghulam Ahmad Qadyani claim to be a prophet? What other reasons may be of their being treated to be out of the fold of Islam? Who is the founder of Ahmadiya movement?

Answer: Mirza Ghulam Ahmad Qadyani claimed to be a prophet. According to the Islamic belief, Muhammad (Pbuh) is the last Prophet of Allah and the Qur'an is last of the heavenly Books. Allah says in the Qur'an, "I have made the religion perfect today." Since Qadyanis believe in principles, against the basic teachings of the Qur'an, they are not regarded as Muslims. In order to be a Muslim, it is essential for one to affirm faith in Allah's existence with His attributed names, apostleship of all messengers and prophets sent down by Allah, in finality of prophethood with our beloved prophet—the last prophet day of Resurrection, the Day of Judgement and so on.

Question: The food cooked in the big cauldrons at Dargah Khwaja Moinuddin Chishti (Ajmer) is vegetarian or non-vegetarian?

Answer: It is vegetarian.

Question: Can the funeral prayer be performed in a mosque?

Answer: It can be performed, if there is no other alternative. But it is better to perform it out of a mosque.

Question: It is believed that Allah commands things to be and it is Allah who commands. Why did it then take six days to create the heavens? Wasn't it created in one go?

Answer: Everything comes to push as Allah wills. The Qur'an mentions the event of creating the heavens. There is no doubt in it. We should bear it in mind that many things are of symbolic nature in the Qur'an. Their narration may also be figurative. At the same time, it is also a fact that human beings are still working hard to unearth different layers of the meanings of several verses and words of the Qur'an.

Question: Why are the Muslims called terrorists? Are all terrorists Muslims?

Answer: No true and good Muslim can be a terrorist. It is not at all fair to brand all Muslims as terrorists.

Question: Some people say that it is a forbidden (haram) act to recite the verses of the Qur'an with food or some eatables in front of one. They believe that such eatables are also forbidden for one to eat. Do such people deserve to be called Muslims?

Answer: I have already answered a similar question, elsewhere in this book. Nevertheless, an answer is here. It is not bad to recite some verses of the Qur'an for seeking Allah's forgiveness on behalf of the deceased. There is no harm in distributing food and other eatables, among the poor in the name of Allah after reciting some verses of the Qur'an with the eatables in front of one.

Question: Allah says that He leads one to the right path and causes one to stray. When everything is done by Allah, why should a man be held responsible and accountable, at all?

Answer: Allah has endowed human beings with rational minds, so that they can distinguish between good and bad. Allah also teaches man what is good and what is bad through the Qur'an. He has clearly pronounced as to who is on the right path and who is on the wrong, who is from among those, who earn Allah's good pleasure and who are from among those who incur His wrath. What Allah says here means the declaration of His absolute power. But it never means that He will not let a good Muslim to follow a righteous path. Allah is kind and merciful.

Question: In what language was the Qur'an initially written? Who wrote it? What are the fundamental teachings of the Qur'an?

Answer: Revealed in the Arabic language, it was committed to pen by the honoured writers of wahy (revelation of the Qur'an). According to the instructions of Prophet Muhammad (Pbuh), the fundamental teachings of the Qur'an include that Allah is the creator of this universe. He created human beings from a pair of a male and a female. He will take the account of every human being on the Day of Judgement. Every human being is from among the children of Adam and Hawwa (a.s.) and Adam was made of clay, while Hawwa (a.s.) was made born from the rib of Adam (a.s.). So, no one has preference over others on the basis of language, race, colour, caste, etc. The best in the sight of Allah is he, who is the most righteous and Allah fearing. Allah sent down His commissioned prophets and messengers to all communities, with the messages for their guidance. Adam was the first human being as well as the first prophet. And Prophet Muhammad (Pbuh) is the final prophet. Similarly, the Qur'an is the last heavenly Book sent down by Allah for the guidance of human beings. The Qur'an explicitly says that there is no compulsion in the matter of religion. It also declares that those who believe in other religions, let them follow their religions and those who believe in Islam, will practice their own religion.

Question: What does Islam say about playing cards, chess, flying kites and so on? Are they forbidden?

Answer: All such games and playthings which make people neglect their duties towards Allah and the responsibilities towards societies are forbidden. But if people are mindful of their duties towards Allah and the society, they can participate in sports for entertainment and maintenance of physical and mental health. But, betting is strictly forbidden.

Question: Which places in India are worth visiting for the Muslims? Why is Haju, a place near Guwahati, famous among the Muslims?

Answer: India is a vast country with hundreds of sights and places of great social and religious significance. One can only name a few, for instance: Ajmer, Delhi, Agra, Fatehpur Seekri, Aurangabad, Hyderabad, Mysore, Srinagar, Cherar-e Shareef. Haju is famous for a saint's mausoleum.

Question: Muslims, Christians and Jews are the descendant of Prophet Ibraheem. Muslims distinguish between the lawful and the forbidden things as prescribed by the Qur'an and the prophetic traditions. Do the Christians also distinguish between the lawful and the forbidden as strictly as the Muslims? Does the Bible make any mention that the Christians eat pork? I have heard that the original Bible has been yielded to corruption, and the Christians do not strictly follow the teaching of Hadrat Isa (a.s.) or Christ. It is also said that Allah has Himself undertaken the responsibility of safeguarding the Qur'an from corruption. What are your views?

Answer: There are clear demarcations between lawful and unlawful things in the scriptures of the Christians and the Jews as well.

Question: Request for raising funds for mosques, as also for financial assistance for other good causes are made just after the performance of a Friday prayer. As a result, supplication (dua) is delayed and the number of people participating in supplication is pretty less. It is said that the votaries of prayer are required to stay in the same condition after the termination of prayer. Is it correct or incorrect?

Answer: It is not against Islamic ruling to go away from the mosque after the performance of a prayer. It is a good act to participate in a congregational supplication. But it is not integral to prayer. However, one should also take care of the discipline, while going out of the mosque after the termination of a prayer. A mosque is Allah's house. One is required to maintain discipline and conduct oneself well over there. Prophet

Muhammad (Pbuh) said that the votaries of prayer should remain seated in the same posture for a little, after the termination of a prayer.

Question: Should we recite Bismillah before reciting Durood?
Answer: We have been commanded to recite Bismillah before beginning any work. But there is no such instruction for the recitation of Durood.

Question: Most of the prayer mats have the pictures of the Holy mosques or atypical mosque. Isn't it forbidden for us to perform our prayer on such mats? Our act of standing on these mats amounts to disrespect of the mosques. If it is not proper to perform a prayer on such mats, why isn't the sale of such mats checked?
Answer: The pictures of the holy mosques are on the part of the mats where the votaries of prayers prostrate. Thus, it does not amount to disrespect of the holy mosques.

Question: Some people sound Salwat after Azan to call the votaries of prayers for the performance of prayers. Is it correct in the light of Qur'an and Hadith?
Answer: The Muslims at some places sound Salwat after Azan. I think, nothing is wrong in it.

Question: Can we greet drunkards, gamblers and fornicators?
Answer: One is supposed to severe one's relationship from the drunkards, the gamblers and the fornicators. If they are socially boycotted, they may be brought to the right path.

Question: Where are the holy graves of Hadrat Adam and Hawwa (a.s.)?
Answer: There is no authentic information about the location of the graves of Hadrat Adam and Hawwa (a.s.). But there are some Sami books which mention the existence of the graves of Adam and Hawwa (a.s.) on the earth.

Question: Some fanatic Hindus believe that if the Muslims drink water from the sangam (point where two rivers meet), they will become Hindus. Is it correct? Why aren't such fanatic Hindu organisations banned?
Answer: If it had been so easy for people to become Hindu or Muslim just by drinking some specific water, there would have been no need of the reformers and religious leaders to disseminate their messages. The belief rests in one's capability to distinguish between the right and the wrong, as it is also in one's spiritual power and exemplary character. There are some so-called Hindus who believe that they are the protectors of their religion.

They terrorise not only the Muslims by their statements and some gestures but also the people of other religions. Fortunately, those people who believe in human values stand against such things and frustrate the plotting of the fanatics. We know it very well that we have to obliterate terrorism from every field. We should be mentally, educationally and socially be well aware of the fact that terrorism is a public menace.

Question: The Qur'an says that for those who are believers and are intelligent (also), there is a life in retribution. The Qur'an also says that these people will not go against it. What does it mean?

Answer: The verse of the Qur'an referred to, by you occurs in Suratul Baqarah. It has a historical background. This law came as a law against the cruel and ruthless attitudes of the Arabs against one another. If a person of one tribe was killed, the relatives of the victim used to kill many people of the murderer's tribe. There used to be ruthless violence in the society. In view of curbing the ruthless violence, Islam prescribed three conditions: 1. If the revenge for murder is murder, it implies that law of equality is prescribed, *i.e.*, blood for blood. But it does not mean that the killer must be killed in the same manner as he killed the victim. It only implies that there has to be retribution of the same nature as inflicted upon the victim and the assassins will be put to death as punishments. It is called Qisas (retribution). It is significant to mention here that in the pre-Islamic days, people used to give their slaves or some weak people for the revenge of murder to be executed on them. It was a cruel practice.

2. Killing a person is an encroachment upon human rights in the sight of Islam. Initially, Islam does not want the killer to be put to death as in a revenge exacted on the killer. If revenge brings solace to the avenger, it inflames the feelings the relatives of the killer put to death in revenge. Islam says that the killing of a killer may have its benefits but it is better to save a life by giving one a chance to improve. Islam is so broad-minded that it gives preference to the individual's rights over the rights of the state. It also has the scope for forgiveness. If the heir of the person killed wishes to forgive by accepting blood-money, the killer may be exempted from the death punishment. The blood-money is called '*dait*'. The Qur'an prescribes no amount of blood-money. But according to some Hadith, it can be one hundred camels or an amount worth the cost of same. But the heir of the person killed has the right to forgive him by accepting even less.

3. However, the best way is to forgive the killer. Prophet Muhammad (Pbuh) had forgiven the blood of his uncle Hamza on the occasion of his farewell pilgrimage to the holy house of Allah.

Question: Some Muslims celebrate the day of *Shab-e-Barat,* as a major festival. While on the other hand, some Muslims call the celebration as *shirk* and *bidat.* What is your opinion?

Answer: The expression '*Shab-e-Barat*' means the night of redemption and deliverance. We should seek Allah's forgiveness for the deceased. We should also pray to Allah for forgiveness and bring ourselves to sincere repentance. It also provides us with a fair chance to remember the deceased and remember our own deaths.

Question: Some Muslims prepare Halwa (sweetmeat) on the 11th of Jamadil Awwal and 14th of Shabanul Muazzam. They recite some verses of the Qur'an with the sweetmeats kept in front of them. This practice is known as *Niyaz.* Is it lawful according to Islamic *Shariah*?

Answer: Everyone has a right to lead his or her lives with particular religious practices. The pillars of Islam are: Belief in oneness of Allah, Allah's messengers, the life thereafter, and belief in the Qur'an to be a divine Book, as also affirming faith in Prophet Muhammad (Pbuh) to be the last prophet and messengers of Allah. If one's practices do not contradict the basic articles of faith, one can practice them in the light of any of the interpretations and with good intention.

Question: According to the Qur'an, Hazrat Ibraheem took Hazrat Ismaeel (a.s.) for sacrifice in the path of Allah. But according to the Bible, it was Ishaq (a.s.) whom Hazrat Ibraheem took for the sacrifice. What is your opinion?

Answer: According to the Islamic belief, it was Ismaeel (a.s.). Hazrat Ibraheem was 90 years old when Hazrat Ismaeel was born to Hazrat Hajra, the wife of Hazrat Ibraheem. He was the first child. We have unwavering belief in the Qur'an.

Question: Is using a verse of the Qur'an as an amulet permissible? Some people write some verses of the Qur'an on plates in ink or saffron and give the needy to wash into water and drink. It is believed to work like some medicine for the patients. Is it permissible? Importantly, those who write verses for amulets have no knowledge about the meaning of the verses.

Answer: The Qur'an is a Book of guidance for perfect and ideal way of life. It is a perspicuous light for those who fear Allah. It benefits one as much as one applies its teachings in one's actual life. It is the miracle of the Qur'an that its verses serve as a potion as well. But its verses should not be sold in the form of amulets.

Question: Those who believe in Allah are obliged to worship Him. Are they also obliged to conduct themselves well with others?

Answer: It is obligatory for every Muslim to worship Allah and conduct himself well with others. One can never be a true Muslim unless one follows Allah's commands and the traditions of Prophet Muhammad (Pbuh), sincerely. As for worship, it teaches us to surrender ourselves with servitude to Allah. On the other hand, it also teaches us to create harmony and peace in the society. If one is deficient in worship of Allah, one may be forgiven by Allah. But one will not be forgiven by Him, if one has hurt anyone verbally or physically unless the person hurt, forgives one.

Question: In my village, there are two mosques. One of them belongs to *Brailawis*. Can a Sunni perform prayers led by a *Brailawi*?

Answer: We can perform our prayers led by any leader of the prayer. The leader is required to be a believer in the oneness of Allah and worshipper of none but Allah, without associating any partnership with Him. His ways of life should not be against the teachings of Islam. It is unfortunate to treat any Muslims with certain reservations. It brings ill reputation to both Islam and the Muslims.

Question: The Muslims belonging to the school of thought commonly known as *Ahl-e-Hadith* do not follow any of the four Imams. But they call themselves Sunni. Whom do they follow?

Answer: They are from among the Sunni Muslims. They do not follow any of the four Sunni Imams. They emphasize that the Muslims should believe and follow what the Qur'an says and what the traditions of the Prophet (Pbuh) teach. They follow Imam Taimiyah, Ibn-e-Qayyam and Imam Shukani. It is pertinent to mention here that all Sunni Muslims follow the teachings of the Qur'an and the traditions of the Prophet (Pbuh). Importantly enough, the differences in opinion exist because of the interpretations of the verses of the Qur'an and some Ahadith.

Question: Normally, Shias and Sunnis perform their five daily prayers in separate mosques, earmarked for them. Doesn't it imply that they are divided into two sects?

Answer: They are two different sects. But all Muslims can pray in whichever mosque they like. The existence of two different mosques does not mean that there are some differences in their fundamental beliefs.

Question: If someone reads the translations of the verses of the Qur'an, will he get the same rewards that one gets for reciting verses in the Arabic language?

Answer: According to our belief, the Qur'an is the holy Book of Allah. Its recitation earns one a lot of rewards. At the same time, it is important for the believers to understand the meaning of the verses in order to know what Allah expects from us. One can't reckon the benefits that the Qur'an contains for human beings. Obviously, reading the translation of the verses of the Qur'an also has numerous merits.

Question: Allah sent down more or less one lakh twenty four thousand messengers for the guidance of the humankind. Are there any books which contain the names of all those messengers?

Answer: There is no such book that contains the names of one lakh twenty four thousand messengers. Every Muslim is required to believe in all the messengers of Allah sent down before Prophet Muhammad (Pbuh). The names of a few messengers find mention in the Qur'an as well.

Question: There is a mosque where first the Muslims belonging to Brailawi school of thought pray on Friday and then those belonging to Deobandi school of thought. Is it allowed to sound two Azans, deliver two Friday sermons and perform two Friday prayers in the same mosque?

Answer: The Prophet (Pbuh) of Allah taught people the art and importance of living together with mutual co-operation. It is Allah who knows the innermost desires and it is He who accepts and rejects one's worshipful acts.

Question: Tell me something about Hadith. What kinds of sinners will they be considered who object to some Hadith?

Answer: The term Hadith refers to sayings and doings of Prophet Muhammad (Pbuh), as also the statements and the deeds of his companions that received silent approbation of Prophet Muhammad (Pbuh). The Qur'an expects us to live an exemplary life strictly based on its teachings. The life of Prophet Muhammad (Pbuh) is the only perfect and ideal model life, in full conformity with the teachings of the Qur'an.

Question: Did Prophet Muhammad miss the time of any of his five daily prayers? Was the prayer, *tahajjud* obligatory for him?

Answer: As recorded in some books, he missed the time of some of his prayer while coming back from the battle of khandaq. *Tahajjud* prayer was obligatory on him.

Question: Are there other books, except the Qur'an and books containing the Hadith, which aren't concerned with any schools of thought like Shia, Barailawi and Ahl-e-Hadith?

Answer: Besides the Qur'an, books of *Ahadith* compiled by Imam Bukhari are the most authentic books. These books are also known as *Sahi Bukhari.*

Question: Who were *Quraish*? What kind of conflict did they have with Prophet Muhammad (Pbuh)?

Answer: Quraish was the name of a tribe in Makkah. It combined many extended families. *Banu Hashim*, the family to which Prophet Muhammad (Pbuh) belonged. He was the most prominent and integral part of this tribe. Many people of the *Quraish* tribe opposed him because he propagated the messages of Allah – His oneness, belief in the Qur'an, the day of judgement and all other basic articles of faith. Those people who opposed him, said that they didn't want to abandon the path of their ancestors.

Question: Will one's act of slaughtering a sacrificial animal ensures one's deliverance and redemption?

Answer: No one's act of slaughtering a sacrificial animal will ensure one's deliverance and redemption. It is an expression of one's close and intimate relationship with Allah. According to our belief, neither blood nor the flesh of an animal reaches Allah. One's act of slaughtering a sacrificial animal is accepted by Allah before one actually slaughters it. As regards flesh, we have been commanded to distribute among ourselves and use it as food.

Question: I have not studied Arabic and Urdu. Tell me an easy way to learn the Qur'an. What is the correct way of affirming intention of Friday prayer? Which one is correct – Aslam walaikum or Aslam alaikum?

Answer: You must seek the help of a Hafiz for learning how to recite the Qur'an. One should affirm one's intention in the following way: I affirm my intention to offer two cycles of prayer of a Friday prayer, for Allah, facing Kaba as my direction and under the leadership of this Imam. Assalam alaikum is the correct expression.

Question: Tell me something about Allah's existence and His attributes? Where does he live?

Answer: According to the Qur'an, there is nothing like Allah in this world. Thus, He cannot be compared with anything. His attributes cannot be described and captured by human beings. As it is not possible for us to describe His attributes, similarly, it is beyond human mind to know His dwelling place. As explained in the Qur'an, it can only be said that He lives on ninth heaven and is closer to a man than his jugular vein.

Question: Are only Muslims permitted to perform Sunnat and Nafl prayers? Can Hindu perform Sunnat and Nafl prayers in their homes for getting the reward of prostration? Where can one get a book which teaches how to perform Sunnat and Nafl prayers?

Answer: Allah says in the Qur'an, "Except such as have faith and do righteous deeds, join in the mutual enjoining of the Truth, and of patience and constancy, others are in loss". (*Surah: Al-Asr*). These words of the Qur'an are not for Muslims alone but for all human beings. Now one must see, if one has these merits or not. The ways of worship or prayer are either prescribed by religion or as per the religious traditions. One should worship according to the ways prescribed by one's religion. The books on the ways of performing namaz are easily available with book sellers dealing in Islamic literature.

Question: The mausoleums of Muslims and the temples of Hindus are generally situated by the roads on controversial places which inflame communal disputes. Is it appropriate?

Answer: The mausoleum or the temples which are there from time immemorial are the symbols of our spiritual heritage and identity. It is not at all befitting for us to nurse some doubts about their genuineness.

Question: It is said that the graves of Hadrat Shees and Hadrat Nooh are in Ayodhya, Faizabad, (Uttar Pradesh). I have visited these graves situated on the way from Ayodhya to Faizabad. Is there any proof in any books regarding these graves? Is it proper to believe in it?

Answer: There is no authentic historical proof of these graves. But some people believe them to be there. Nothing can be said about them with authenticity.

Question: Islam, Christianity and Judaism were preached by people who descended from the same lineage. Is it true? Please tell their family tree.

Answer: It is true that the preachers of Islam, Christianity and Judaism were the people who had descended from the same great grandfather, Hadrat Ibraheem who is also known as Abraham. Ishaq (a.s.) is from among the children of Hadrat Ibraheem. And Hadrat Moosa and Hadrat Isa traced their lineage with Ishaq (a.s.). They were the propagators of Judaism and

Christianity respectively. Prophet of Islam Hadrat Muhammad (Pbuh) traced his lineage with Ismail (a.s.), another offspring of Hadrat Ibraheem. It is mandatory for Muslims to believe in all the prophets. It is pertinent to mention that according to the Islamic belief, it is Allah who is the creator of the universe. He alone is the sustainer of the world.

Question: In case a child offers the obligatory prayer standing between adults, will the prayer of the adults become invalid? Passing before a person who is praying is forbidden. If some one wants to pass, what should he do? Will a woman's ablution be invalidated after she feeds her child?

Answer: It makes no difference if a child offers his prayer standing between adults. But, as per the tradition, the children should stand behind the adults. One can pass before a votary of payer if there is a sort of object like a pillar, wall or stick, etc., in front of the votary of prayer. It is called *Sutrah*, a symbolic barrier between the votary of prayer and others. It should be one foot in height and over an inch in width. In case there is no such barrier, one should keep sitting in front of him until he finishes his prayer. Ablution of a woman is not invalidated after feeding her child.

Question: Both Shias and Sunni are Muslims. Then, why do they fight? They do not accord respect to each other's sacred places and do not go for intersect marriages. I have one more question. If Islam believes the God to be present in every particle of the world, why doesn't it accept the presence of God in idols? During Hajj Muslims kiss '*Sang-e-Aswad*'. Isn't it idol worship?

Answer: It is a matter of great sorrow that some of the followers of Hadrat Muhammad (Pbuh), who was the embodiment of love, peace, amity and tolerance, are involved in such inhuman activities. Such persons have nothing to do with Islam. They do so for serving their own ends. It is not proper to say that they do not go for intersect marriages. You can see lots of examples of such marriages. No doubt, according to Islam everything bears witness to the presence of God. He is closer to us than our jugular veins. But he does not exist inside something. He is on the ninth heaven. It is beyond the capacity of human being to describe and capture His greatness, glory and His abode. There is nothing in the world which He can be compared with. According to Islamic belief, only He deserves to be worshipped. There arises no question of worshipping anyone else other than Allah. During Hajj, a pilgrim does not worship *Sang-e-Aswad*, the black stone. Thus, kissing of *Sang-e-Aswad* is a part of circumambulating Kabah. It is the same as a Muslim's prostrating with his nose and forehead on the earth. But the prostration is not for the earth itself. It is for Allah alone. There goes a famous saying of Hadrat Omar, the second caliph of Islam. He said while addressing the black stone that he would not have kissed it, if he had not seen his master Prophet Muhammad (Pbuh) kissing it because it was simply a stone.

Question: You say that one can watch T.V. and go to the cinema. Are these acts permissible for one who follows Islam? Can you cite some Hadith in favour of it? Are the rewards of the acts like fasting and five daily prayers curtailed, if these acts of worship become *makruh* (nearly forbidden) due to certain acts?

Answer: According to the Islamic belief, no other act than the acts of worship need some validation and substantiation from some previous traditions. However, we need to give argument for not doing an act. Scientific inventions are not intrinsically lawful or unlawful. The important thing is the way one makes use of them. Of course, they may be used in a good as well as in a bad way. For example, there are different types of programmes on T.V. which are not ethical. The Muslims are prohibited from watching them. We have a logical reason to prove that they are not good enough for the society. Similarly, there are good programmes too. We are not prohibited from watching them. Allama Yusuf-Al-Qarzavi, a big contemporary expert of Islamic laws, is of the same opinion. *Makruh* means undesirable and near forbidden. A votary of prayers and one who observes fast run the risk of suffering curtailment of rewards on account of not being fully attentive to various acts that these major acts of worship involve.

Question: What is *Aab-e-kausar*? When will it be available to people, in the world or in the world after?

Answer: Kausar is the name of a canal in heaven. There is a mention of it in Hadith. *Aab-e-Kausar* or water will be whiter than milk and sweeter than honey. On the Day of Judgement Prophet Muhammad (Pbuh) will offer its water to quench the thirst of the people of his community.

Question: The Muslims wash hands and feet for obtaining cleanliness before the prayer. Why do they first wash hands and then feet? Is there scarcity of water in India? When asked, the Muslim brothers say that people have to give the account of every drop of water. Is it true?

Answer: To make the life balanced, Islam has set the bounds for everything. There should be an appropriate use of water for obtaining cleanliness too. Government propagates, 'water is life'. We pray five times every day. It is not easy for us to take a bath before every prayer. But one who needs may take a bath. Since you do not know about the etiquettes of ablution, you think that it is not correct to first wash hands and then feet.

Question: There is a mosque only 50 metres away from the market. But some persons in the market do not go there and pray in congregation in the market itself. However, there is no sectarian difference with the people on the mosque over there. Is it proper?

Answer: The prayer of the persons praying in the market will be accepted but it will be better, if they pray in the mosque.

Question: Is it a virtuous act to make Tazia, to bring it to the procession and to bury it every year? If it is an act of virtue, why there is no tradition of Tazias in Saudi Arabia? The Prophet of Allah Hadrat Muhammad (Pbuh) was in Saudi Arabia. Please explain in the light of the Qur'an and Hadith.

Answer: There is no reference of Tazia in the Qur'an and Hadith.

Question: The whole world knows that Allah is omnipotent and the Creator of the universe. Why at all He could not force Satan to prostrate? Allah ordered and the Satan disobeyed in spite of being a creature of Allah.

Answer: Allah has given a limited liberty to human beings, Jinns and Satan. On the Day of Judgement, a strict account of their acts will be taken. On that day the humans, Jinns and Satan will not have the courage to disobey Him.

Question: Allah is '*Hazir* and '*Nazir*' too. I can understand 'Hazir' (present) but what is the meaning of 'Nazir'?

Answer: 'Nazir' is a word of Arabic language which means one who can see.

Question: It is said that Islam is against caste system. Is it proper for the Muslims to take the reservation facilities on the caste basis? Idol worship is prohibited in Islam. Is keeping hair of Hadrat Muhammad (Pbuh) in Hazrat Bal some kind of idol worship?

Answer: Islam does not accept caste system. But it is a bitter truth that the social system in India is quite different. Due to local influence, the caste system has become the part of Muslim society too. The decision of reservation is a political compulsion more than a social and economic need. How can you blame the Muslims for it? As far as keeping of hair from the beard of Hazrat Muhammad (Pbuh) at Hazrat Bal is concerned, people visit see it. They do not worship it.

Question: What is the meaning of *Tazia*? What do some Muslim try to convey on the occasion of Muharram by beating their chests and wounding their bodies? Who started the tradition of *Tazia* and when?

Answer: The word *Taziat* means to console and to express one's grief. But it also stands as symbol of the grave and the mausoleum of Imam Husain. It is not made by using gold and silver plates, but bamboo sticks, cloth and paper. This comes to symbolise grief, sadness on the occasion of Muharram. Sometimes, it is taken in a procession but sometimes, it is put in houses, Imam Baras and on some specially raised platforms which are known as Imam Sahab Ka Chowk. Historically speaking, Aziz Billah Fatmi of Egypt observed *Yom-e-Husain* (day of Husain) for the first time in 977 AD. After that it was observed in different regions in various ways. It led to the tradition of making *Tazia*. Inflicting one's body with some wounds during the practice called *Matam* (mourning) is more social than a religious tradition. It shows their commitment towards Imam Hussain. It also shows that they can bear any pain for him.

Question: How can we get an in-depth knowledge of *Fiqh*? Does Shia sect accept the famous books of Hadith (Sehah Sita)? If they do not accept it, tell the name of the collection of Hadith compiled for them.

Answer: You can get an in-depth knowledge of *Fiqh* from a scholar of Islam or from the books published on this subject. Generally, Shias do not accept all the Hadith of Sehah Sita. They have some collections of Hadith. '*Kaleeni Shareef*' the is most famous collection among them.

Question: To which Sufi chain did Hazrat Nizamuddin Auliya (r.a.) Khwaja Bakhtiyar Kaki (r.a.) and Moinuddin Chisti (r.a.) belong? Who became their successor? Tell in detail about the Sufi order.

Answer: All these Sufis were associated with Chishti order of Sufis. Khwaja Moinuddin Chisti of Ajmer, is the foremost preacher of this Sufi order in India. His disciple and successor was Khwaja Qutbuddin Bakhtiyar Kaki. His mausoleum is in Mehrauli, Delhi. The successor of Qutbuddin Bakhtiyar Kaki is Baba Fariduddin Ganj Shakar (r.a.) whose mausoleum is in Pak Pattan, Pakistan. His Sufi songs are integral part of Guru Granth Sahib, the sacred book of Sikhs. Farid Kot, a city in the State of Punjab, is named after him. The disciple and successor of Baba Farid was Mahboob-e-llahi Khwaja Nizamuddin Auliya. He is also called, the 'Emperor of Delhi'. The successor of Nizamuddin Auliya is Shaikh Nasiruddin Chiragh Dilli (r.a.). A big area of Delhi is known as Chiragh Delhi. His mausoleum lies there only. Hazrat Chiragh Dilli's chain goes to south India and reaches to Banda Nawaz Gesu Daraz. His mausoleum is in Gulberg Shareef. It is to date a centre for guiding light to the Sufi traditions.

Question: If someone listens, someone taking the name of Prophet or someone himself pronounces the name of the Prophet Muhammad (Pbuh), then it is compulsory to recite *Durood.* Why is it recited? In order to send it to Allah?

Answer: Allah has commanded us to invoke His blessings onto Prophet Muhammad. This command comes to us through the Qur'an. It is an expression of our devotion and attachment with the Prophet of Allah. It is also done in order to obey Allah's command. Allah is our creator and we sing the glory of Allah through various acts of His worship.

Question: If there is some controversy or a court case pending against a mosque, will the prayer performed there be accepted by Allah?

Answer: To accept or reject one's prayer is solely on the will of Allah. But one is not prohibited from praying in such mosques.

Question: A chadar (sheet of cloth) is offered to cover a saint's grave. After some time, it is taken away by someone from the management committee of the shrine. It is a matter of surprise that it is sold back to the same shopkeeper, who had sold it. What will happen, if some other devotee purchases the same chadar and offer it to cover the grave? Is such a person who offers the same chadar for the second time be considered to have committed some sin?

Answer: You may contact the people associated with some Dargah's management committee.

Question: There is an analysis of the Qur'an in '*Satyarth Prakash*', a book written by Swami Dayananda Saraswati. It is said in this book that one who does not affirm faith in basic articles of Islam is a *kafir.* In this way, every one except the Muslims is a *kafir.* Explain the meaning of word '*kafir*'.

Answer: The analysis of the Qur'an presented by Swami Dayanand Saraswati is based on his personal thought and understanding. One who denies the truth is called a *kafir.* It is the greatest lie to deny the existence of the creator of the universe, falsify His messages and the prophets sent down by Him. The Qur'an says that Allah sent down His messengers with divine messages for the guidance of the people belonging to every community. It must be kept in mind that the Qur'an clearly declares that there is no compulsion in the matter of religion, as 'your religion is for you and for me is mine. It proves that those persons who blame that Islam exerts pressure in the matter of religion are not speaking truth. More importantly, Swami Dayananda Saraswati criticised every religious traditions including those of Hinduism. So, his thoughts should not be analysed in reference to Islam alone.

Question: Some persons (like some terrorists) misquote Hadith to justify their wrongdoings. Due to this a sort of misunderstanding about Islam has creeped in. What should the Muslims do in this regard?

Answers: The misuse of the prophetic traditions for serving one's personal interest and ends is permissible for one under no condition. Those who commit such acts are guilty in the sight of Allah and His Prophet (Pbuh). It is the responsibility of every Muslim to wisely avoid injustice, exploitation, oppression or any evil act in the name of the Qur'an and Hadith.

Question: According to Islamic traditions and teachings, one's entire body needs to be clean before offering a prayer. Since the entire body is made from a dirty drop, which part of the body should be treated clean and which one dirty?

Answer: No doubt, human body traces its origin in a filling drop. But it does not mean that one should remain dirty from birth to death. Cleanliness is an integral part of the faith of the Muslims. Islam has the etiquettes of ablution and bath prescribed for the people. They are obligatory. Needless to say, cleanliness also protects one against several ailments.

Question: My husband used to get scared during sleep at nights. But now he is obsessed by the fear during the daytime as well. He is so frightened that he does not prefer to close his eyes. He does not feel inclined to perform his daily prayers also. Prescribe me some Surahs of the Qur'an which may cure his ailment like this.

Answer: Whether or not you feel inclined towards performing five daily prayers, these are compulsory. He should first be punctual to five daily prayers, then recite these *Surahs: Kafiroon, Ikhlas, Mulk, Naas* and *Ayatal Kursi* and blow over him before going to sleep. Allah willing, he will be cured.

Question: In response to a question you said that the reward of any act depends on one's intention. If every thing depends on the intention, why should people be caught by the religious rituals like offering Salah, fasting, Hajj, pilgrimage to holy places, Arti, idol worship and so on? Does Allah need His slaves to flatter Him? I practice none of the rituals mentioned above. But I do my work diligently and honestly. Cannot all persons remain only humans? It is necessary for people to accept the worn out religious traditions and be identified as the Hindus and the Muslims?

Answer: Perhaps you did not read my answer with reference and context. Good intention is necessary in performing the daily prayer. One needs to have right intention for fasting, Hajj and Zakat also. These acts have spiritual as well as practical aspects. They have positive influence on the life as well as the society. Performance of five daily prayers reminds the votaries of prayer the background and the purpose of their creation, makes them duty-conscious, builds their character and personality, lets them have conquest over the their self, coaches them into discipline and punctuality, lends them the power of following the leaders and fosters a sense of equality and brotherhood. Fasting gives those who fast a sense of servitude to Allah, builds character, lends them phenomenal power of patience and perseverance, and lends them spiritual advancement. They are also able to realise the hunger and thirst of a poor person. Similarly, the dispensation of Zakat helps the poor and helpless rise above poverty line. During Hajj pilgrims rise above the mundane feelings of colour, caste creed, region and language. They come together at one place and demonstrate a civilised and cultured behaviour. It shows our complete surrender and unity, and ways of religious rituals, spirit of sacrifice, gives us lesson of unity and brotherhood. The creator of this universe needs no sycophancy. Both Hindus and Muslims are human beings. The religious beliefs help them become better human beings. If a person is not a good human being, he can neither be a good Hindu nor a good Muslim. You may subscribe to a particular religious belief but one's being an active and a good human proves one's relation with religious belief and system of life. Shri Krishna said in the Geeta that one should do one's work and should not bother for the result.

Question: Is it permissible for one to wear a watch with iron and steel strap or a bracelet during performance of daily prayer?

Answer: It is permissible for one to wear a watch with an iron or steel strap during the performance of daily prayers.

Question: It is said that to walk on the path shown by Prophet Muhammad (Pbuh) is to walk on the path of Allah and the hand of Prophet

Muhammad (Pbuh) is the hand of Allah. The words of Prophet Muhammad (Pbuh) are the words of Allah. Is it true?

Answer: Prophet Muhammad (Pbuh) led his life in conformity with the commands of Allah. Allah has clearly commanded us to follow the command of Allah and the teachings of His Prophet (Pbuh). Obviously, the acts of following the ways of the Prophet will earn one Allah's rewards.

Question: Sunni Muslims offer *chadar* to the graves of saints. They also perform the acts known as Niyaz and Fatiha. Are these acts allowed in Islam?

Answer: The Muslims belonging to all sects visit mausoleums. The act of associating partner with Allah is '*Shirk*'. I do not understand how the act of Fatiha can be branded as *Shirk*.

Question: According to you, preaching is a tradition of the prophets. Can you name any prophets who went to the Muslims to propagate Islam and stayed in some mosque during their journey, as is practised by the people associated with Tableeghi Jamaat.

Answer: All the prophets preached their faith. Certainly, they preached the faith among the people they were sent to.

Question: Prophet Muhammad (Pbuh) is the leader of all prophets and friend of Allah. We have got the *Kalima* and the Qur'an through him only. But the Qur'an also mentions the names of Hazrat Isa, Hazrat Moosa, Hazrat Daud and Hazrat Sulaiman. Did Prophet Muhammad (Pbuh) came to narrate the tales of the past prophets? If so, how can he be called their leader?

Answer: No doubt, Prophet Muhammad (Pbuh) came to complete the religion that was brought to the people by Hazrat Adam. He is not the founder of a new religion. As far as the leadership of the prophets is concerned, Prophet Muhammad (Pbuh), he led the prayer performed by all the prophets as followers at Baitul Muqaddas on the occasion of his celestial ascension (*meraj*). This is why he is also called "Sayyadul Anbia" and "Sayyadul Mursaleen".

Question: I am a teacher in a Sunni Madrasa in Khalilabad, Uttar Pradesh. Some Aalim at the Madrasa says that one should not fold the bottoms of one's pants/pyjamas inside out. While on the other hand, the Ulema, belonging to Ahle Hadith and Deobandi schools of thought are of the opinion that pants or pyjamas can be rolled up inside out. What is your opinion?

Answer: According to a prophetic tradition, no male Muslim is allowed to cover his ankles by the length of his pants/pyjamas.

Question: It is said that the prophethood of Hadrat Muhammad (Pbuh) was declared after 40 years of his age. And he was given five times Salah as a gift from Allah on his celestial ascension. Which Salah did Prophet Muhammad (Pbuh) perform before his celestial ascension?

Answer: Before the declaration of his prophethood Prophet Muhammad (Pbuh) used to retire in the cave of Hira. He used to sing Allah's glory and worship Him with total devotion to Him. Salah is a form of worship which was made obligatory on the Muslims on the occasion of the Prophet's (Pbuh) celestial ascension. Prophet Muhammad (Pbuh) established Salah and taught us the method to perform it. It was made obligatory with its prescribed times and cycles of prayer.

Question: What was the religion of Hadrat Umar Farooq before he embraced Islam?

Answer: The people belonging to the Quraish tribe who were the residents of Makkah, believed in the True religion (Deen Haneef) preached by Hazrat Ibraheem (a.s.). But when Prophet Muhammad (Pbuh) was sent down by Allah among them, they were no longer steadfast believers in the religion preached by Ibrahim (a.s.). Hazrat Umar Farooq was one of those people.

Question: There are basically two sects, Shia and Sunni. There is a wide difference between them. They are also hostile to each other. If someone wants to embrace Islam which of these two sects should he choose?

Answer: Of course, there are two major sects, namely Shia and Sunni. They differ on the opinion regarding *Khilafat* and *Imamat*. But they are not hostile to each other. Ayatullah Khumeini and several other Shia scholars contributed a lot towards bridging the gulf between these two sects. The reason of the conflict between them is not religion but other issues. As regards a neo-Muslim, it should be left to his option. He should be free to choose whichever sect he likes.

Question: What is the meaning of Islam? Can we define Muslims in the light of the definition of Islam?

Answer: Islam means full surrender and total submission to the will of Allah. It also implies peace. Submission to the will and command of Allah refers to an ideal way of life by which peace can be established on the earth. According to Islamic belief, Allah is the Creator and the Lord of the universe. He alone knows what is good and what is bad for human beings. This is the reason that the way of life prescribed by Islam is the most perfect and ideal way of life. Islam claims that the things and acts forbidden by Islam are injurious to an individual as well as to the society. And things permitted by Islam are beneficial for an individual as well as for the society. A Muslim can be branded as a good Muslim or as a deviant Muslim in view of his practices and conduct. What is beneficial for people is permissible and what is injurious to them is forbidden?

Question: According to the Qur'an and Hadith, the Muslims should help the needy, whether Muslims or non-Muslims. Hinduism also attaches great importance to the service of human beings. Why on the earth, the Muslims and the Hindus fight among themselves? Obviously, the poor Muslims and poor Hindus both are the sufferers.

Answer: I agree with your opinion. None of the two religions can be blamed for the conflict between the Hindus and Muslims. It is all engineered by the people motivated to gain political mileage. The people with your opinion can play a very good role to strengthen the relationship between the Hindus and Muslims.

Question: Some people pronounce as 'Walad-Duallean' and some as 'Walaz-zaulleen'. Which one is correct?

Answer: The pronunciation of two Arabic letters (dha) and (da) are in a way identical, if one does not have a proper training to pronounce these two phonemes he can make a mistake. This is the reason that we are required to recite the Qur'an on the Arabic phonetic line.

Question: Munkir-Nakeer will appear in the graves of dead people to frighten them. How will they frighten a blind man, as they will not be visible to the blind?

Answer: The faith that *Munkir-Nakeer* will frighten the dead is not in conformity with the Islamic belief. *Munkir* and *Nakeer* are two angels of Allah. They appear in a grave for some questions and answer session. It is believed that those who have done good deeds, will be happy to see them but those with bad deeds will get worried.

Question: I am a businessman. I don't live in my locality during the appointed time of prayers. So, I do not pray Salah in the mosque near my house. I pray in other mosques. Will my prayer be valid?

Answer: It is valid to pray Salah in any mosque.

Question: There is a tradition in India to recite the verses of the Qur'an while putting the food items in front of one. People do so with an intention to send the rewards to their dead ancestors. Is there any indication to it in the Qur'an or Hadith? Can it be substantiated in the light of Qur'an and Hadith?

Answer: I have answered similar questions, elsewhere in this book. I say again that although the tradition continues to be it in India and somewhere else, yet there is no evidence in the Qur'an and Hadith to substantiate the ways of such types of practices. But giving food, clothes or water on behalf of the departed ones is a form of charity. It will earn them rewards. It can be substantiated with the Hadith which describes about a companion of Prophet Hadrat Saad who asked him, "My mother has died, what should I do to earn Allah's rewards on her behalf." The Prophet (Pbuh) said, "Get a well dug and dedicate it to the people on behalf of your mother. As long as the people will drink water from the well, she will continuously get the rewards." All the schools of Fiqh unanimously agree with it. As regards the ways of Niyaz practised by people, there is no consensus among the scholars of Islam.

Question: When Prophet Muhammad (Pbuh) went on the celestial of ascension, his followers got the gift to perform five daily prayers. What type of celestial ascension it was?

Answer: The celestial ascension is that journey which Prophet Muhammad (Pbuh) undertook. He was taken to Baitul Muqaddas from the place where he lived a night before his celestial ascension. He had his celestial journey from there. According to Islamic beliefs, he reached the places where no one else, not even an angel had got the access. There Allah gave him some instructions which included the performance of five daily prayers obligatory for the Muslims. The celestial ascension conveys us the message that exalted heavens and their vastness are not away from human reach. The condition is that one should have firm faith in oneself as well as in Allah.

Question: It is an Islamic belief that nothing happens without the will of Allah. Do the riots, wars, bloodsheddings and natural disasters, etc. take place according to Allah's will?

Answer: It is an Islamic belief that all the creatures are under Allah's control. So, nothing happens without the will of Allah. But the Creator of the Universe has also made a general principle for the world that whatever happens here is the result the actions of human beings. We should see the disasters in this context only. We should also have it in the mind that Allah does not help the community which does not help itself. Man gets from Allah for what he makes efforts.

Question: Is it proper for a Hafiz to take money in the month of Ramazan for Taraweeh? People contribute thousands of rupees and give him as a token of his leading the prayer.

Answer: If the votaries of prayer voluntarily give money, it is permissible for a Hafiz to take it. But fixing the amount like a businessman is not proper.

Question: When and how did the tradition of circumcision begin? What is its importance in Islam? If an adult is converted to Islam, is circumcision mandatory for him?

Answer: Hadrat Ibrahim (A.S.) got himself circumcised at adult age. Circumcision is his tradition and is mandatory for every male Muslim, provided that he does not have any physical problem. It is useful for health from medical point of view.

Question: The Muslims belonging to Barailawi sect call the Muslims of Deobandi sect *kafir*. The Deobandis call Barailawis *mushrik*. Where should a neutral Muslim pray – in a Barailawi or in a Deobani mosque? People say that Prophet Muhammad (Pbuh) prohibited the Muslims from branding each other as *mushrik*.

Answer: Do not get involved in such conflicts. Be impartial and pray in whichever the mosque is situated near your house. At the time to offer prayer, pray wherever you are. Allah gives reward of our worshipful acts on the basis of one's intention. The difference between Barailawi and Deobandi scholars lies in the interpretations of certain verses of the Qur'an and some sentences of Hadith. They all believe in the same basic articles of faith.

Question: "O Prophet! strive hard against the unbelievers and hypocrites, and be harsh with them. Their abode is Hell – an evil refuge (indeed)." "Verily, the unbelievers are your enemies'. Do these verses really exist in the Qur'an? If yes, why is there so much hatred towards other religions? According to the Islamic teaching, those who do not believe in Allah and His Prophet (Pbuh) are *kafirs*. Should we wage Jihad against them or should we consider them our enemy?

Answer: The verses mentioned by you occur in *Surahs* 66 and 4 respectively. They are conditional and were revealed to the Prophet (Pbuh) for the guidance of the Muslims under special conditions. For example, the word 'unbelievers' occurring in the verse 66 refer to those people, who perpetrated cruelties and indignities on the Muslims in Makkah as well as in Madinah. Their hostilities were escalated to an extent beyond human toleration. They were bent upon obliterating the Muslims from there. Their survival was not possible without encountering with these people. By a general consensus among the scholars of Islam, it is believed that this command was not meant to be applied to the general unbelievers. It was applicable only to those who were perpetrating violence on the Prophet (Pbuh) and his companions. Prophet Muhammad (Pbuh) had made a pact with the followers of all religions, including the idol worshippers, in Madinah. According to it, everyone had the right to follow and practice his religion and solve the disputes according to the laws based on his religious traditions. As far as hypocrites were concerned, they were the ones who pretended to be Muslims. They had animosity against Islam in their hearts. They lost no opportunity to harm the Muslims and Islam. So, it was necessary to take action against them. As regards verse 4, you have not quoted it completely. If you had read it properly, you would not have asked this question. The meaning of this verse are: "When you are a traveller, you will earn no sin if you shorten the prayer, or if you fear that the adversaries of your religion will perpetrate ruthless cruelty on you, verily, the adversaries of your religion are your enemies." The Qura'n says, "There is no compulsion in the matter of religion." It further says, "To you is your religion and to me is mine". This is the moot point. If we believe in these principles, we can create a society where people of different sects and religions can co-exist with their traditions amicably.

Question: The study of the Bible shows that the prophets showed miracles, made forecasts and told about future, revealing their knowledge about the unseen. They did so because they wanted to prove their authenticity as prophets. Prophet Muhammad (Pbuh) showed no miracle, why should we accept him as the Prophet and the Qur'an as a heavenly book?

Answer: A miracle is showed by a prophet by the will of Allah. But the most important thing is his life and character, as also the message carried by him. One who has read about the life and character of Prophet Muhammad (Pbuh) will not raise this question. The Qur'an, heavenly message of Allah to His slaves, is itself a miracle of the highest order. Everything contained in the Qur'an is still intact in its pristine form. It is recited and heard by millions of the votaries of prayer in Traweeh prayer in the month of Ramazan. You should spare some of your valuable time to read the Qur'an and about some biography of Prophet Muhammad (Pbuh). It will dispel all doubts and confusions.

Question: Allah says in the Qur'an, "To you have We granted the abundance. Therefore, to your Lord, turn in prayer and sacrifice". According to the Qur'an, we have to perform our daily prayers after drinking from *kausar.* Some Ulema say that one will be made to drink from *kausar* after one's death. What comes first in order of precedence – prayer or *kausar*?

Answer: Our real merit consists in the spirit of expressing gratefulness to Allah. We should worship Him with total loyalty because He created us in the best of the moulds and made us His representative. Those who strive hard for being the true representatives of Allah, will earn Allah's rewards. *Kausar* is one of Allah's rewards.

Question: According to Islam, Allah created the earth. What material did He use to create the earth? Who created Allah?

Answer: According to Islamic belief, Allah created not only the earth but also everything the universe contains. No one created Him nor begot Him. He is neither a son nor a father. Allah is eternal and exists by Himself. With all His attributes of perfection, He will continue to exist even when everything will be perished.

Question: Is participation in a competition where prizes are given, a sin? When one combs hair, one has one's some hair detached. Similarly, when one trims one's nails, one has to cut the unwanted parts of the nails. Are the women obliged to bury or throw their hair detached from their heads, and such parts of nails into rivers? Is it a major sin to be intentionally late after hearing the call for the prayer? Is it also a sin to start making ablution or going for a bath after the call for prayer is sounded?

Answer: It is not necessary for them to throw the hair and parts of nails into the rivers. Since nails have no nutritional value in them, if some animals eat them, they may develop T.B. This is the reason that our elders advise us to bury them. It is not at all good for one to be intentionally late for the prayers. It is entirely a different matter, if one is late due to one's engagement in ablution or bath. These are compulsory acts.

Question: Since the funeral prayer consists of no bowing (*rukoo*) and prostration (*sajda*), some people don't consider it a prayer. What is your opinion?

Answer: Prophet Muhammad (Pbuh) commanded us to perform the prayer the way the votaries of prayer saw him perform. So, we have to perform a prayer as Prophet Muhammad (Pbuh) performed it. He performed funeral prayers without bowing and prostration, so we also perform funeral prayers without bowing and prostration.

Question: According to the Qur'an, all men and women from Adam to the last person born on this earth before the doomsday, will be resurrected on the Day of Judgement. Will this earth be able to accommodate all of them? As guessed by people, a space measuring 25 yards will accommodate 25 lakhs of people. Is it possible? Isn't it the Bible and Qur'an's declaration that all the people who were born, will be resurrected and made to stand on the same plane, something ridiculous?

Answer: There are several descriptions in these heavenly Books. Many of them are metaphorical. It is not proper to treat them to be something like a mathematical formula. There are wonderful inventions and discoveries by virtue of science. We encounter with new things everyday. Maybe some day or the other, we are able to unravel many wonderful secrets of nature. Before two hundred years, it was supposed to be merely a wild imagination to fly in the space and use air-conditioners. But now they are facts. Similarly, the revolution in the world of communication has made the world a global village. It is important to note that everything in the universe will be disintegrated on doomsday.

Question: I have heard that Prophet Muhammad (Pbuh) was not very handsome. That is why he did not allow anyone to make his picture or sketch. Is not it true?

Answer: The books containing Hadith and Islamic history describe his unparalleled handsome features and inner beauty, which have also been praised highly by friends and foes alike.

Question: The Qur'an uses the words 'Maula', 'Rab' and 'Allah'. Are these three words synonymous or these differ in meanings?

Answer: 'Maula' means 'master' and 'Rab' means 'sustainer'. These are the attributes of Allah.

Question: Christians, Muslims and Jews make a claim on the city of Jerusalem (now in), Israel. What is the basis of their claims and how is city sacred and significant for the Muslims?

Answer: Jerusalem is one of the oldest cities of the world. According to the history, Hadrat Yaqoob (A.S.) constructed here a place of worship named 'Baitul Muqaddas'. One thousand years before the birth of Isa (a.s.), the place of worship reconstructed and the city was rehabilitated on the order of Hazrat Daud (a.s.). Baitul Muqaddas and nearby areas were also the centre of the preachings of Isa (a.s.). Prophet Muhammad (Pbuh) undertook his journey for celestial ascension from this place. It finds mention in Surah Bani Israel in the Qur'an. The Qur'an says, "Glory to Allah Who did take His servant for a journey by night from the sacred mosque to the farthest mosque…". (*Surah: Bani Israel, Verse:* 1). Initially, Prophet Muhammad (Pbuh) and his companions faced Baitul Muqaddas to perform prayers. Prophet Muhammad (Pbuh) migrated to Madinah from Makkah. After some time, they started praying with their faces towards Kaba. That is why for the Muslims Baitul Muqaddas is the third most sacred place after Makkah and Madinah. It should also be kept in mind that the Muslims believe in all the prophets including Hazrat Yaqoob, Hazrat Daud, Hazrat Suleman, and Hazrat Isa.

Question: Allah is called 'Rahman and Raheem'. Can He forgive one who neither prayed one's five daily prayers nor fasted during the month of Ramadan? What should one do if one has missed one's prayers for 50-60 years? How is it possible for one to pray these missed prayers of one's?

Answer: According to Hanafi school of thought, one should make a rough calculation about the missed prayers from the time, when prayer became obligatory for one. One should pray one's obligatory missed prayers with one's five daily payers, likewise *witr* with everyday *witr*.

Question: What is the historical background of the sacred hair of Prophet Muhammad (Pbuh) kept in Hazrat Bal Dargah, Kashmir?

Answer: I have earlier, answered a similar question. As recorded, Prophet's hair was kept there in 1111 Hijri, corresponding to 1700 AD. Hazrat Syed Abdullah brought it from Madinah in 1046 Hijri to Bijapur (India). When his son, Syed Hamid, came to Jahanabad for some work, Nooruddin Eshawari, a businessman from Kashmir, took it from him. Aurangzeb took the sacred hair from him to be placed in the Mausoleum of Khwaja Moinuddin Chishti. Being struck by the grief of losing the sacred hair, Nooruddin Esawari died. Hearing the sad demise of Nooruddin, Aurangzeb permitted a companion of Nooruddin, Khawaja Moinuddin, to take the sacred hair to Kashmir. In Kashmir, first of all, it was put at Khanqah-e Naqshbandi and it was finally shifted to Bagh Sajid Khan, presently known as Hazrat Bal.

Question: Are prayers still offered in Masjid-e-Aqsa? Is this mosque in the occupancy of Israel?

Answer: Prayers are still being offered in Aqsa Mosque. It is in the occupancy of Israel.

Question: The Muslims follow one Qur'an, one Prophet and the same basic articles of faith. Why do they have several sects? Which sect do you think is on the right path?

Answer: No doubt, the Muslims follow one Qur'an, one Prophet and the same basic articles of faith. Such types of differences or sectarianism are also found in other religions as well. It seems to be something natural. According to Islam, differences are constructive and positive. Needless to say, the differences of opinion bear witness to the democratic values. The differences do not concern the basic articles of faith. They are primarily due to the interpretations and explanations. The basic articles of the beliefs are the same. As far as the differences between Deobandi and Brailawis are concerned both of them belong to Sunni Hanafi school of thought. Their differences originate from explanations. As regards a sect being on the right path, the Prophet (Pbuh) said that the merits of one's act lie mainly in one's intention. It is Allah alone who knows the innermost feelings and intentions of people. So, no human being reserves the right to brand some one good or bad.

Question: Is visiting mausoleums is *shirk*? Can the acts of making *Tazias* and taking them to a procession on the occasion of Muharram be branded as *shirk*? Are auliya alive in their graves? Were they just like us?

Answer: The act of associating some partner with Allah is known as *shirk*. One's acts of visiting a mausoleum to offer *fatiha*, offer floral tributes, and pray to Allah cannot be branded as *shirk*.

Question: The laws for the Muslims in India, on the basis of their personal laws, are different in several matters. It had been proper, if there had been different criminal laws for them as well. It is not good that they have the same criminal laws which every other citizen of India has.

Answer: The rules of law for the Muslims in India based on their personal law serve the purpose. There was a consensus among the member of constituent assembly that there should be common criminal laws for all citizens of India. We should respect the consensus and agree with the decision.

Question: On some occasions like Thursdays, the birth day of the Prophet (Pbuh) I purchase some sweets and distribute them among people. But I do not recite any *Surahs* for the purpose of *Neyaz* and *Fateha*. Do such acts earn the pleasure of Allah?

Answer: Allah knows the intention. All the acts done with sincerity and things dispensed for earning His pleasure will bring Allah's rewards. It is not necessary to have days and the method fixed for good acts.

Question: It is said that the real '*bahishtee maqbarah*' is in the graveyard of Qadiyan. The other maqbarah '*zille bahishtee maqbarah*' is in Khwah, Pakistan. The third '*bahishtee maqbarah*' is in Bakhehee, London. Has '*bahishtee maqbarah*' been built as the gate to heaven? Qadyanis are called Ahmadiyas too. They claim themselves to be Muslim. Are people trapped by them due to lack of education?

Answer: All these are baseless. They have nothing to do with Islamic beliefs and concepts.

Question: When did Islam come to India? Who brought it? Some people say Islam came to India from Arabian countries or with Khwaja Moinuddin Chishti? What is your opinion?

Answer: Islam came to India with Arab traders. These Arab traders were active in Kerala, at Konkan coast and Gujarat. After the conquest of Sindh by Muhammad Bin Qasim, some Muslims settled in this area. Data Ganj Bakhsh in Lahore promoted the tradition of Sufism before Hazrat Khwaja Moinuddin Chishti and Khwaja Moinuddin himself devoted forty days of devout worship of Allah with total servitude to Him. Chishti Sufi tradition, brought by Khwaja Moinuddin Chishti in India, played a very important role in the propagation of Islam in northern India.

Question: Is the prayer performed with yawn valid? Will the prayer be valid if one prays in a room with a T.V. on? Will one's ablution be invalidated, if one happens to see some *namahram* or a wedding procession?

Answer: The prayer is valid even if one yawns during prayer. It is better for one not to pray in a room with a TV on. If there is no option, and the TV can't be switched off, one can pray within this room. The ablution is not invalidated after seeing a *namahram* or a marriage procession.

Question: I have a brother who prays to Allah but does not work. Sometimes his wife and children have to starve. When we question his ways of life, he says that Allah is Sustainer and the Master. Is his prayer true? Or, is it some kind of hypocrisy?

Answer: There is a clear distinction between rights and duties. There are some duties that one has towards Allah and some towards common people. One is obliged to do one's duties which one owes to human beings. If a person performs his duty towards Allah but ignores his duties towards others, he is openly acting against the instructions and commands of Allah and His Prophet (Pbuh). If one is deficient in one's duties, towards Allah, He may forgive one because He is the most benevolent and most merciful. But if one is deficient in performing one's duties towards fellow human beings, Allah will not forgive for it until the affected person forgives. It is clearly stated in the Islamic teachings that the closer is a person, the greater is his right. The Qur'an clearly warns us that man reaps the result of his actions.

Question: There is a woman who always fights with her husband, tells lies and does not respect her in-law, she is illiterate and does not know how to pray and fast. Does the Qur'an permit her husband to divorce her on these counts?

Answer: The husband must have been in the know that the girl is illiterate. As far as her behaviour and lifestyle are concerned, the husband must contact his wife's parents and her siblings to get her ready for the desirable ways of life as prescribed by Islam. It won't be proper to divorce her on these counts. We should not forget that the divorce is the most detestable permissible act in the sight of Allah. We should also consider the psychology and future of the children who are born out of the wedlock.

Question: I took an oath by the Qur'an a month earlier that I would not smoke. But just after a week, I again started smoking. Now every person makes me feel ashamed. They ask me to expiate. How should I expiate?

Answer: It is a highly irresponsible act. You should not have sworn by the Qur'an. Anyhow you have to expiate for it by feeding 10 poor people. If you are not financially able to feed the poor, you should fast for three days, pray and seek Allah's forgiveness.

Question: Is it a sin to use the devices for preventing pregnancy for the sake of family planning? If one suspects that there may be some life-threatening complications, is one allowed to get the pregnancy terminated?

Answer: The use of devices for birth control is not bad. But if one fears that one will not be able to provide basic amenities of life to the children, it is not proper. It is so because Allah is the Creator and Sustainer as well. According to the jurists of Islam, one can get the pregnancy terminated only if one has a life-threatening risk.

Question: Don't you see any shortcomings in Islam? Do you have any hesitations in discussing them? The weaknesses are: (a) marriages in intra families (b) eating and drinking in the same utensils with fellow Muslims at the same time. According to modern science and other religions, it is unhealthy and unhygienic. But Islam says that such practices beget love between people. What is the status of woman in Islam? Is she a commodity? Aren't the acts of fixing the dower at the time of Nikah to be paid by the bridegroom and the payment of dower at the time of divorce, something like paying money for the chastity of the bride?

Answer: We have a firm belief that whatever Allah prescribes for us keeps us away from every type of evils. As regards marriage in intra families, it has several advantages and merits. The sociologists have discussed them in detail. Further, it is not necessary for one to go for intra family marriage. As far as sharing food in the same utensils is concerned, it has its own etiquettes. Special emphasis is given on the cleanliness. According to Islamic beliefs, cleanliness is an integral part of the faith. The same kind of question was once asked to Hazrat Nizamuddin Auliya. He replied that people might eat in the same utensils at the same time, if the food items did not contain gravy. However, the reason behind eating together in the same utensils is that it begets love among people. In Islam man and woman have equal status. Generally, Allah addresses both males and females together in the holy Qur'an. Islam grants more rights to women in comparison with men. Islam does not allow its followers to consider women as commodities. As regards dower (*mehr*), it intends to ensure economic security to the married women. If a woman is unfortunately divorced, the dower given to her will economically support her at the time of divorce.

Question: What is the Islamic injunction about taking a photograph and keeping it?

Answer: According to the general opinion of scholars of Islam, it is not good to take and keep photographs. However, it is permissible under certain conditions. However, a religious verdict regarding photographs was given by Mufti Muhammad Abdahu, the disciple of Jamaluddin Afghani, in 1896. The verdict said that photographs would not lead to idol worship because human minds have now developed a lot. So, people think that there is no harm in taking pictures. Shaikh Yusuf Al Qarzavi, a great contemporary scholar of Islam, is in favour of taking pictures.

Question: Some women do not fast during the month of Ramazan at the pretext of their menstrual cycle. Are they allowed to do so?

Answer: They are not allowed to fast during their menstrual period. They will compensate the missed fasts after they obtain purity.

Question: What is *Halal*? On Eid-ul Azha Muslims kill innocent goats. Is it right?

Answer: Allah is the Creator of the entire universe and everything it contains. He knows better, what is good for humans and what is bad for them. Islam prescribes for people what is good for them as well as for the society. Whatever is prescribed by Islam is permissible (halal). Similarly, the things which are harmful for them are forbidden by Islam. Things forbidden by Islam are *haram.* Islam ensures rights to animals as well. But the things which are the part of human food, should be eaten in a way that guarantees health to people. That is why it is only proper to slaughter the animals in a prescribed way. Medical science recommends that the use of the flesh of animals slaughtered as per Islamic ways is healthful. We must bear in mind that the knives should be very sharp so that the animals have to bear the minimum pain. Importantly, we should not flash the knives in front of the animals. As far as Eid-ul-Azaha is concerned, it has a special message. The act of slaughtering a sacrificial animal gives us a message that we must be ready to lay down our lives for upholding the truth.

Question: What is *Aqeeqah*? Why it is done for boys only? Is it mandatory for the rich and the poor alike?

Answer: When a baby, a boy or a girl, is born to the Muslim parents, they express their thankfulness to Allah by offering sacrificial animal (s) in the path of Allah. It is in consonance with the prophet's tradition.

Question: Is it possible for one to have the faith of the highest order which is known as '*Ainul Yaqeen* and *Haqqul Yaqeen*'? If it is possible, what are the ways?

Answer: One can attain every type of faith in this world, provided that one has sincere intention, complete and firm faith, combined with continuous strivings. Allah helps those persons who are armed with these qualities.

Question: My mother died approximately 10 years ago. Then, we were very young and were not home. We attended the funeral ceremony. Now we want to do something for her. What can we do for her now?

Answer: According to a prophetic tradition, the act of a virtuous child to invoke Allah's blessing through his prayer is one of those things that reach the deceased. You can pray for her forgiveness, securing a better place and rank in heaven.

Question: What is the meaning of *Fatwa*? Is it a sinful act to ignore a *Fatwa*?
Answer: Etymologically, the word '*Fatwa*' is an Arabic word. Its plural is '*Fataawa*'. Literally, it means munificence and kindness, as also power. In Islamic terminology, it refers to the verdict given by a jurist (faqeeh) of Islam. In common parlance, it also stands for the answers to the questions given in the light of the Islamic rulings.

2
Social Questions

Question: Some Hindu girls, who enter into marriage with Muslim boys, affirm their faith in the basic articles of Islam at the time of their marriage. Similarly, some Muslim girls who happen to marry Hindu boys also convert to the religion of their husbands. Islam does not deem the marriage of a Hindu girl with a Muslim boy valid without the girl's affirming faith in the basic articles of Islam before marriage. It is also quite common that some Hindu girls after their love marriage with the Muslim boys practice their own religion. In other words, the wives worship their idols and their husbands perform their five prayers daily, observe fasts and perform other religious rituals also. Are these marriages valid according to Islamic laws?

Answer: Good and bad deeds depend on an individual's conscience. As regards, Islamic laws it does not allow people to maintain such relationships.

Question: The people associated with Tableeghi Jamaat propagate Islam in consonance with the prophetic traditions. But some people belonging to Barelvi school of thought claim that people associated with Tableeghis are not on the right path of Islam. Is it true? If Tableeghis preach Islam in consonance with the prophetic traditions, why do Barelvis say so?

Answer: As far as I am concerned, I uphold and support the objectives of Tableeghi Jamaat. The Muslims cannot reach consensus on any matter except for the belief in Allah's existence, His perfect attributes, apostleship of Prophets sent down by Allah and the Heavenly Books. In view of it, one can say that differences of opinion should not make us anxious.

Question: Do prawns and crabs form permissible or forbidden seafood? Some say that prawns are the worms of the body of Hazrat Ayyub (a.s.). People say, when Hazrat Ayyub took his bath as per the command of Allah, these worms wriggled out of his body to swim in the water.

Answer: According to Hanafi rulings, only fish, from among sea creatures is permissible for one to eat. Prawns are nearly forbidden. It is forbidden (haram) to eat other sea creatures. According to Shafaee school of thought, all sea creatures are permissible. But the story you quoted about the prawns is concocted.

Question: I, a Commerce graduate, am 21 years old and non-Muslim, I have a good job. I am in love with a working Muslim girl. We have been living like husband and wife for three years. But now the girl says that she will marry a man from among her own religious fold. So, now I am ready to embrace Islam. How can I embrace Islam?

Answer: Contact Darul Qaza, Okhla, New Delhi.

Question: Hindus, Sikhs, Jains, originally belonging to India hold the cows to be sacred. But the Muslims and the Christians, who once migrated other countries slaughter them. They do not understand the importance of cows, though they are very important for human beings. Isn't it possible for the Muslims and the Christians to avoid slaughtering cows for the sake of amity, peace and harmony?

Answer: As regards, slaughtering the cows, it is important to mention here that no cow is slaughtered in the states where the cow-slaughter is banned. But for the states where cow-slaughter is not banned, the Muslims and the Christians are not to be blamed for the cow-slaughter.

Question: I, hail from a scheduled tribe, and am a Hindu youngman. I want to convert to Islam, but my wife does not want to convert. Can I marry a Muslim girl after my conversion?

Answer: Conversion to any other religion depends on one's own conscience and one's ability to distinguish between right and wrong. It is not allowed to use allurement or pressure of any sort. After one's conversion to Islam, one can marry any Muslim girl. According to rules and regulations, only those from Hindu religion are considered from scheduled caste and scheduled tribe.

Question: I am a 20 years old Dalit young man. I do not regard myself to be a Hindu. I am in love with a Muslim girl and want to convert to Islam. Will the Muslims accept me?

Answer: Conversion to religion is permissible, provided that there is no compulsion, allurement or threat. Conversion to religion is solely a matter of one's own conscience and inner voice.

Question: What are the pre-conditions, for one to convert to Islam? If a non-Muslim converts to Islam, will he be able to find suitable matches for his children?

Answer: The most important condition for one, who wants to convert to Islam is that one should not yield to allurements, threats or compulsions. Instead, one should follow the dictates of one's conscience and inner voice. If one's children also convert to Islam, one will find suitable matches for them in Muslim families.

Question: On the demand of my wife, I divorced her before one year. She had no contact with me during her three menstrual periods. As a result, the contract of marriage was terminated. My six years old son lives with his mother at his maternal uncle's house. They do not let me meet him. Does Islamic Sharia permit one to meet one's son?

Answer: You did not mention the reason why your wife demanded you to divorce her. However, according to a prophetic tradition, divorce is the most detestable permissible act in the sight of Allah. Since you pronounced only one talaq and you did not establish relationship with your wife during three menstrual periods, you can re-enter into the marriage, if you both wish so. You can meet your son without any condition. Islamic Sharia permits it. I think you should better find some intermediary for a graceful solution to the problem. Of course, the court will also restore you your right.

Question: Islamic code of dress includes skull cap. But you are not wearing the one?

Answer: Thank you very much. You drew my attention to it. With due respect, I wish to tell you that it is not an obligatory duty to wear a skull cap. I do wear it on certain occasions.

Question: Is it obligatory for one intending to pay pilgrimage to the holy house of Allah to meet one's relatives with whom one does not have good relationships?

Answer: Hajj is a duty that a Muslim owes to Allah. It is essential for one to perform one's duty towards one's relatives and fellow human beings. If there are some issues between him and others, he should try his best to resolve them.

Question: In the present day world the Jews, the Jains and the Buddhists in general are prosperous. On the contrary, the Muslims are poverty-stricken. What are the reasons?

Answer: Prosperity and poverty have nothing to do with a particular, caste race or region. One is not rich or poor due to ones association with a particular religion. It is an undesirable fact that those, who work hard with firm determination regularly and understand the demands of time are successful.

Question: What should one prefer, one's religion or one's country? The Muslims prefer their religion to their country. Is it the reason why some Muslim cricket fans celebrate the victory of Pakistan over India?

Answer: Your question sounds to be incorrect. It is like asking one, if one loves one's children or one's mother. There is no religion that teaches its followers to do some thing against the interest of their country. For the Muslims', love for their country, is an integral part of their faith. If one makes a survey of the existence of different religions in the world, one will find countries with citizens belonging to different religions and faiths. Even Pakistan has the Christians, Hindus, Parsis and Sikhs as its minority communities. Pakistan can ask them to be patriotic to their country. So, there is no conflict between the basic articles of faith and patriotic feelings. If an Indian Muslim celebrates the victory of Pakistani team over Indian team, it amounts to foolishness. It has nothing to do with religious sentiments.

Question: Today, the Muslims are faced with illiteracy, unemployment and poverty, what are the solutions? What measures have been taken in respect of warding off or minimising their problems?

Answer: Yes, they are faced with several critical problems. But I am of firm opinion that one can solve one's problems by virtue of one's hardwork and good perseverance, and also resolute faith and trust in Allah. Needless to say, every problem has different types of challenges. But every problem comes with equally good opportunities. According to the meaning of a verse of Qur'an, Allah does not better the condition of a community that does not pay sincere heed to its condition and feel genuinely concerned about the betterment of its condition. As an individual, I have been whole heartedly engaged in the mission of motivating people and infusing them with confidence and hope to brave the challenges with steadfast resolution to emerge victorious.

Question: I have been living in a rented house without paying any amount as advance. Now the owner wants me to vacate the house. He is ready to give me one lakh and fifty thousand rupees, as an incentive to vacate the house. Is it lawful for me to take the money from him?

Answer: It is not permissible for one to take such money. Even ethics do not allow such acts.

Question: It is mentioned in some books that husband and wife should not keep away from each other for more than four months. If the husband stays away from his wife for more than four months for earning his living, is it allowed or not?

Answer: According to the Islamic laws' it is not permissible for one to stay away from one's wife for more than four months. But by mutual consent, the spouses can stay away for earning their livelihood.

Question: What should a Muslim do against the cruelties perpetrated on others?

Answer: A Muslim is required to do what Prophet Muhammad (Pbuh) has said. According to a prophetic tradition, there are three grades of Iman: First consists in one's countering the tyranny with full might and power. Second consists in one's act of open condemnation of the tyranny. Third consists in one's act of degrading it. Once Prophet Muhammad (Pbuh) said, "Help your brothers whether they are tyrant or oppressed". Listening to this the companions of the Prophet said, "We can understand the meaning of extending help to the oppressed but we do not understand how one will help the tyrant. Then Prophet Muhammad (Pbuh) said, "You should help the tyrants by stopping them from perpetrating tyranny."

Question: Does Islam give some rights to the neighbour? If it gives, does a non-Muslim neighbour also deserve those rights?

Answer: Islam prescribes unparalleled right to the neighbours. According to a saying of Muhammad (Pbuh), if one does an evil act to a neighbour, one earns manifold sins. According to another saying of Prophet Muhammad (Pbuh), he is not a Muslim who eats his fill but his neighbour remains hungry. Moreover, one is not allowed to discriminate between a Muslim and a non-Muslim neighbour.

Question: People say that the principles of Islam are egalitarian. But in practice one does not see these qualities in Muslim society. Why is it so?

Answer: You have touched the crucial nerve of the Muslim society. We can't deny the fact that the caste system is prevalent among the Muslims in the subcontinent. But the fact is that it is just opposite the spirit of Islam. No one is either superior or interior on the basis of race, caste and colour. According to Islamic Shariah and Islamic faith, all human beings are the slaves of Allah and the children of Adam. Since, Adam was made of clay, no one has any superiority over others.

Question: According to the Qur'an, women are the tilth of men. Doesn't it mean that women are the property of menfolk and they have no social rights?

Answer: The verse that you have mentioned here does not mean it. Tilth means that women perpetuate the family. It does not mean that women are the property of menfolks. As the earth is important for farming, women are important for the promotion of human race. Islam has given more rights to women than men. According to Islam, the paradise for a man lies under the feet of his mother. The act of bringing up two female children well will earn the parents a place in paradise.

Question: Will the women who are disobedient to their husbands be admitted to heaven? What kind of treatment will they receive in the life hereafter?

Answer: Any one who disobeys Allah's injunctions regarding the observance of one's duties towards one's spouse, will face a dire consequences in the life hereafter. Allah knows the best as to who will be admitted to heaven and who will be thrown into hell.

Question: If some Muslims are subjected to some kind of oppression, the Muslim leaders make a lot of hue and cry. But they keep silent, when the Hindus are subjected to cruelties. Why is it so?

Answer: I do not agree with your point of view. One may have differences of opinion with the Muslim leaders but one can't say that they are apathetic to the cruelties perpetrated on the Hindus. It is a false accusation. All the Muslim leaders condemned the attack on Akshardham Raghunath Mandir and killing of the innocent Pundits in Kashmir. Syed Ahmad Bukhari, Imam, Jama Masjid, Delhi, appealed the Muslims to fight against the terrorists in Kashmir. The reason why the true feelings and concern of the Muslim leaders do not reach the masses is that their voice does not find space in the media.

Question: If a boy and a girl live like a married couple without entering into the bond of marriage and have children, will the children be deemed legitimate by Islamic Shariah?

Answer: It is a sin to produce children, out of illegitimate relationship. Islam approves of no sinful acts.

Question: Who has a greater status – mother or father? If I am ordered by my mother to do something but I am forbidden by my father to carry out her order, whom should I obey?

Answer: According to Islamic faith, the status of mother is greater than the status of father. As regards obeying father and mother, one has to see the nature of the order. If one's father asks one to do something which one finds to be against the ethics, one should decline. But if he asks one to do something which one finds to be good, one must obey one's father even if one's mother asks one not to obey one's father. But one must try to help one's parents to have such a relationship which is conducive to the growth of a good atmosphere in the house.

Question: When was Darul Uloom Deoband established? What were its objectives? How it is related with Talibani?

Answer: It was established in Deoband on May 30, 1866, in a mosque named Chhattey wali Masjid by a teacher and a student. The teacher was commonly known as Mullah Mahmood, whereas the student was known as Mahmood Hasan. During the struggle for freedom, Mahmood Hasan came to be known as Shaikhul Hind, Aseer-e-Malta. The objectives of this institution included the safeguard of the religious concerns of the Indian Muslims, as also the imparting of Islamic education. Its people took active part in the struggle for freedom from colonial power. It has nothing to do with Taliban. It is possible that some Talibani had studied at this institution before the partition of the country. It is important to mention here that a group of Islamic scholars associated with this institution opposed the division of the country on the basis of religion. Shaikhul Islam Husain Ahmad Madni said, "The foundation of the communities is country, not the religions".

Question: Some women do not observe purdah, when they are out of their homes. But they do observe it, when they are at home. Why?

Answer: Women are required to be modest whether they are out or at homes. Modesty is the ornament of womenfolks. But it is equally important for menfolks.

Question: There are some non-Muslims who want to live in peace with the Muslims. Does Islam teach the Muslims to conduct themselves well with such non-Muslims?

Answer: Islam teaches the believers to live with amity and peace with such non-Muslims. It also commands them to conduct themselves with them. According to the meaning of a verse of the Qur'an, Allah does not prohibit you from conducting yourself well and ensuring justice to those who waged no war against you on the basis of your religion, and did not oust you from your homes.

Question: What was Shah Bano case all about? What was the decision given by the court? Why did it become an issue of conflict?

Answer: Shah Bano, a resident of Indore, was divorced by her husband. She filed a suit in the court for the subsistence allowance. The case reached the Supreme Court from where the jury led by Justice Chandra Chood interpreted a few related verses of the Qur'an and directed her husband to give the subsistence allowance. The interpretation of the verses of the Qur'an gave way to a new conflict. Refusing to accept the Court's interpretation of those verses of the Qur'an the scholars of Islam stood to oppose the verdict of the court. They held it as interference with the Muslim personal laws. It led to a movement. In view of the Muslims' sentiments Rajiv Gandhi led government passed an amendment in the Constitution to quash the verdict of the court.

Question: Dowry among the Muslims is prevalent these days. The brides are subjected to cruelty for dowry. Impart some teachings in the light of the Qur'an and Hadith to check the social abuse.

Answer: Islam allows no dowry in any form. On the contrary, the bridegroom has to pay dower to his bride. Moreover, it is his responsibility to earn his livelihood and provide the necessities of life to his bride. One can cite an example. After his marriage with Fatima (r.a.), the daughter of Prophet Muhammad (Pbuh), Hazrat Ali (k.w.) in accordance with the instructions of the Prophet (Pbuh), sold his armour to host Dawat-e-Walima (reception) and buy some necessary household items. Some practices among the Muslims in the subcontinent trace their origin in the prevalent social customs over there. According to Islam, it is a gross act of sinfulness to subject a girl to cruelty for the sake of extracting dowry.

Question: Generally, Hindus hire a band of musicians on the occasion of marriages. Do Islamic laws allow such a band of musicians on the occasions of marriages?

Answer: It is much better to opt for simplicity and avoid any sort of show of on the occasion of marriages. One does not need flaunt the happiness with the help of the bands of musicians. Such acts are disliked by scholars of Islam.

Question: There are so many sects among the Muslims. They have caste system according to the people's professions. What will the caste of a new Muslim be? Will he be accepted by the people identified by the particular castes? Will he be able to get his children married in these families?

Answer: Islam doesn't believe in caste division. When a non-Muslim converts to Islam, he gains respect and identity everywhere in the Muslim society. He can get suitable matches for his children in the Muslim families. Ideally, he should get the equal opportunity.

Question: A man reserves the right to divorce the women in case she is disobedient and has loose morals. What should a woman do when her husband is of loose morals and is ruthless?

Answer: Islam has given rights to both husband and wife. If a husband can divorce his wife, a wife can also terminate the bond of marriage under unfavourable circumstances.

Question: Traditionally, a bride and a bridegroom are supposed to be at one place for the performance of the ritual of the marriage. Is it permissible for one to enter into marriage with the help of internet and *e*-mail?

Answer: It is permissible, but. The bride or the bridegroom has to appoint a representative who will give the consent on behalf of the bride or bride groom in the presence of two witnesses.

Question: According a report, once, during ragging, some students of Delhi University asked some freshers, a boy and a girl, to take seven rounds. If a Muslim girl is forced to accept some boy in her marriage during a ragging, will it be regarded as a valid marriage?

Answer: According to the Islamic beliefs, marriage without the willing consent of the boy and the girl is invalid. In other words, it is important that the bride accepts the bridegroom willingly.

Question: Is it permissible for a Muslim mason to build a temple?

Answer: People have different professions to earn their living. Raising such question in a country like India, where people of diverse cultures and religions co-exist may be a disservice to Islam and the nation both.

Question: What is the prescribed age for a girl to marry? Should one keep oneself away from one's wife during her menstrual period? According to the Qur'an, the sun and the moon move, whereas according to modern science, it is the earth that moves. Which one is correct?

Answer: According to Islam, the girl should be given into marriage after she attains the age of majority. That is why there is no fixed age. It is forbidden for a man to establish physical relationship with his wife during her menstrual period. The mention of the movement of the sun and the moon in the Qur'an does not mean that they move like the earth. It refers to the diurnal and nocturnal course.

Question: What is your opinion about Muslim girl students wearing modern school and college uniforms and dresses?

Answer: Islam forbids the women to expose their bodies. It has commanded the male and female believers to conceal their concealable parts of their bodies. Obviously, one can wear dresses of one's likings with the restrictions in one's mind.

Question: Twin baby girls were born to a couple belonging to Iran. In the process of the surgery to separate the twins, both of them died. Wasn't the surgery against the will of Allah?

Answer: It was impossible for the parents to avoid the facilities available in medical science. You should also think about daily torture which the girls would be undergoing. We do not consider such remedial steps against the will of Allah.

Question: Boys and girls in Western countries, especially America and Europe, court one another and live closely with each other before their marriages. They believe that by virtue of these things, they will know each other and will have successful married lives. Does Islam permit such a relationship?

Answer: Islam does not sanction such a close relationship between a boy and a girl before their marriage. However, it permits them to see each other before the marriage.

Question: Don't you think that the right of a male to marry four women is against the spirit of equality which women are believed to have? I think four marriages lead to the growth of the population of the country.

Answer: A man is permitted to marry four women at a time under extraordinary conditions only. It is pertinent to mention that it never aims at the exploitation of women. As regards the growth of the population, it may or may not lead to the growth of the population of the country.

Question: Islam allows polygamy. Why doesn't it allow polyandry?

Answer: Islam allows a man to keep four wives at a time provided that he is capable of guarding the interests and ensuring the due rights to all of his wives. It is significant to mention here that it is only for extraordinary conditions. It is not at all a command of Allah. Take for example, the conditions of war between the two countries. The male members of the society are lost. The women outnumber the males. Now the only way to help the widows is to give them into marriage to the married males. It removes the imbalance and checks the gross deeds. In addition to it, one's wife may be infertile. Now it is better for one to marry another woman than to divorce one's first wife and then marry. If one divorces one's first wife for the sake of marriage with another woman, she will be left in wilderness. Islam expects the males that they give due rights to their wives and ensure justice to them. If they are able to stay just with two wives, they can have more than one wife at a time under extraordinary conditions. Needless to say, we have a patriarchal society. It is also seen that many husbands subject their wives to ruthless treatments. If a woman has more than one husband, they will make her life hell. It is only a husband's duty to earn the livelihood. It seems significant to mention here that married women have the right to sue their husband for Khula, a provision for women to terminate the bond of marriage.

Question: The Taj Mahal is one of the wonders of the world. After all, it is a mausoleum. Does it show the short sightedness of the King to spend such a big amount on a mausoleum?

Answer: You may be surprised to know that an Islamic scholar deems its construction fit from the religious point of view. On the other hand, Sahir Ludhianvi, under the influence of the progressivism and socialism, calls it an object that looks down upon the love of the poor and passionate lovers. However, the constructions of palaces and other buildings used to be the source of livelihood of the poor. Several Kings got the tombs constructed but every tomb is not the Taj Mahal. The Taj Mahal is an example of architectural art. I believe one should not see it as wastage of money and the result of short sightedness. One should rather see it as an object of beauty, promoting art and architecture.

Question: There is an old well in front of my house. It is not in use now. The members of my family unanimously think to turn it into a toilet. Is it permissible to do so?

Answer: If the well belongs to you, you can use it the way you want.

Question: Name the women with whom a male can shake hands.

Answer: A male can wish them Salam. As regards shaking hands, there is no such command in Islam.

Question: If one's husband is alive, can his wife go out of her house to work and earn? Is it permissible for him to live on his wife's earning?

Answer: Male and female are equal in the sight of Islam. But the onus is on the husbands to ensure the maintenance of family's livelihood. In case the women are required to work, they can do. But they need to observe the limit set by Islam. And their husbands can use the money earned by them in lawful manners.

Question: If someone says, "Why to give charity and alms to the poor they have been made poor by Allah?" What will be the proper answer to him?

Answer: Giving alms is one of the pillars of Islam. It is obligatory on every Muslim who possesses alms worthy wealth. It is given to the poor by the rich. Dispensary charity has also been emphasised upon, in Islam. Allah says that one who feeds the poor feeds Him. Richness is a means of testing the believers. Allah wants to see how steadfastly a believer spends, from what has been given to him by Him.

Question: Can a woman perform Salah in a standing position? Are there any mosques where women lead Salah? Can you tell the number of girl students learning the Qur'an by heart?

Answer: Like a male votary of Salah, women can also stand to pray. There is an example of a woman leading the prayer of the ladies during the lifetime of the Prophet (Pbuh). I believe there is no mosque where a lady leads the prayer these days. But there are mosques where male and female votaries of Salah pray together with separate arrangement for female votaries of prayer. Since there is no reliable survey available, one can't tell the exact number of girl students learning the Qur'an by heart, but certainly, there are many.

Question: I am 25 years old. I have been earning money for last 15 years. I give my entire earning to my family consisting of my parents and siblings. But after my marriage, there is always some quarrel in the family. I want to live separately with the household items my wife has brought, as dowry. But the members of my family say that they spent money on my marriage. If I want to live separately, I have to pay the amount back, or else they will not allow me to take away the dowry items brought by my wife. Is it permissible for the parents to take back the money spent on their son's marriage?

Answer: Islamic way of life ensures rights to every body. Try to understand the rights of your parents as well as your wife. You owe some responsibilities towards your parents who brought you up. At the same time, you also owe responsibilities to your wife.

Question: I have observed that people distributing sweets in the mosque of my locality prefer the elderly people to the children. Do such discriminatory practices have the sanction?

Answer: Prophet (Pbuh) loved the children very much. He ensured them their rights and admonished his companions and others to take care of the rights due to them. Islamic teaching lays emphasis both on the respect of elders and love to the children.

Question: What does Islam say about the bribe?

Answer: According to a saying of the Prophet (Pbuh), both one who gives and who takes the bribe, deserve places in hell. Islam lays emphasis on both means and ends to be fair.

Question: I am a Homeopathic practitioner. I prescribe biochemical medicines. Is this way of treatment permitted in Islam?

Answer: There is no problem in treating ailments through these medicines. If you think these medicines may be prohibited in Islam because they have too much alcohol, you should also know that alcohol does not remain in its original form when mixed with some other chemicals for the medicinal purposes. If a doctor believes that there is no option left for the effective treatment of a patient and the ailment can be cured only through something prohibited in Islam, he can go for it to save the life the patient.

Question: Is it permissible for a Muslim observing fast to break his fast with the eatables hosted by a non-Muslim?

Answer: There is no harm, if the eatables are not prohibited.

Question: I do not possess a T.V. In view of the revolution in the means of communication and the importance of watching news and good programmes, I want to buy one. What's your opinion?

Answer: There is no harm in watching T.V. for news and informative programmes.

Question: Does Islam forbid one to love a girl?

Answer: No, it does not. But one should love a girl after one enters into marriage with her.

Question: I have a friend. He has portraits of film actors and actresses hung on his walls. Is it permissible for one to do so?

Answer: It is not proper to hang portraits on the walls.

Question: What is the literal meaning of the words Shia and Sunni? What is the fundamental difference between them? When did they emerge as two different sects?

Answer: The word 'Shia' means group. It was initially used for the companions and the followers of Hazrat Ali. Those who follow the path and commands of the Prophet (Pbuh) are called Sunnis. Of course, Hazrat Ali was a staunch follower of the Prophet (Pbuh). Needless to say, all Shias are the followers of the Prophet as well. Thus, one can say that Shias and Sunnis are one. They are divided on the issue of khilafat. It is a political issue. It has nothing to do with the basic tenets of Islam.

Question: Why is washing of the private part compulsory?

Answer: Islam commands human beings to do those things which are healthful for them. Keeping oneself clean is no doubt beneficial for health. And health is the most important of all the valuables possessed by humankind. Islam lays great emphasis on cleanliness. It considers cleanliness to be an important part of the basic tenets of faith. The most important duties of the Muslims include worship of Allah alone, according respect to elders and ensuring equality to one and all. In sum, the Muslims are commanded to lead their lives in perfect harmony with the will of Allah and the traditions of Prophet Muhammad (Pbuh).

Question: Is it obligatory for a Muslim to maintain a beard? Is it obligatory? What should be the length of the beard?

Answer: There is a consensus among the scholars of Islam regarding maintaining the beard. They consider that it is at least a nearly forbidden act to shave the beard. As regards the length of the beard, there is no unanimous consensus among the scholars of Islam.

Question: There are certain Muslim carpenters. They have adopted Saifi as their family title. Is there any harm in adopting Hashmi, Noohi or Najjar as their family title? What is the meaning of Saifi?

Answer: The word 'saifi' has been derived from the word 'saif' which means sword. In fact, Islam does not attach any importance to caste system. A man is superior or inferior by virtue of his belief, deeds, acts of piety and behaviour in conformity with the Islamic Shariah.

Question: According to you 'saifi' means 'sword'. Do you imply that they belong to the group of the people with sword or do you mean that they are from the people who made swords? Is there any mention of the word saifi in the Qur'an or Hadith? Did any messenger of Allah use this word as his family title?

Answer: It is not saifi but the word 'saif' which means sword. Those whose forefathers made arms and tools, call themselves saifi. The word 'saifi' is Arabic but it does not occur in any Hadith bearing this connotation. Khalid bin Waleed was a very brave man. Prophet Muhammad (Pbuh) gave him the title 'Saifullah' (sword of Allah).

Question: Normally, even the educated Muslims also do not practise birth control. Why don't the Muslims believe in astrology?

Answer: It is not fair to believe that Muslims do not practise birth control. The census during the last two-three decades bear witness to the fact that the rate of growth of the Muslim population is not more than the growth of the population of other communities. As regard the second question, according to Islamic beliefs, it is only Allah who is Omniscient. None but He has the power to see the future. Whatever good or bad happens, is caused by Him. This is the reason that the Muslims generally do not practise astrology or consult an astrologer. It is a fact that the Muslims contributed towards the development of science with the help of their study of the universe and constellation of stars. But they did not use it for obtaining the knowledge of their future or destiny.

Question: I have got a sentence written in Sanskrit. It says that good act brings good result and evil deeds yield bad results. The same sentence has been translated into Arabic as well. Hindu and Muslim religious scholars are surprised to see it. Is Islam against Sanskrit or any other language?

Answer: According to Islamic beliefs, Allah sent down His messengers to every community for the guidance of its people. Obviously, each community had its own particular language. Our close study reveals the fact that every language has moral messages. It is full of universal values and thoughts conducive for the growth of humanity. Needless to say, these features of a language are in accordance with the fundamental teachings of Islam. Of course, Islam can never be against any particular language. Moreover, a language has no religion of its own.

Question: My mother's sister wants to get my sister married with her son. But once she had breastfed my sister under some unavoidable circumstances, can she get her married with her son?

Answer: According to Hanafi school of thought, your sister cannot be given into the marriage with the son of your mother's sister, provided that your mother's sister had breastfed your sister during the wearing period. It is so because your sister is the 'razai' sister of your cousin. The term 'razai' refers to one who becomes one's sister or brother on account of sharing the milk of the same mother.

Question: The Muslims, have been facing decline for quite a long time. What are the reasons and the solution? Some leaders believe that it is due to the general weakness of Iman of the Muslims. Is it correct?

Answer: The Muslims all over the world are faced with problems due to the fact that they evade the realities of life and prefer to live in a fools' paradise. It has led to a dangerous situation. Our belief is that whatever good or bad is our share is as destined and also as per the will of Allah. This fact needs to be corroborated with yet another fact that nothing can be achieved without our sincere efforts. According to the Qur'an, Allah does not change the condition of those people who do not change themselves. Of course, supplication is an arm for a true Muslim but it is ineffective in the absence of good deeds. It is a prophetic tradition to eat dessert after one's major meal but it is also a prophetic tradition to tie a stone on the stomach to suppress the hunger pangs. According Prophet Muhammad (Pbuh), there are but two ways of achieving success in life. They are education and business. We will not succeed unless we pay sincere attention to these things. We have to change our habit of separating the worldly matters from our religion. At the same time, it is an undeniable fact that we cannot dream to have a functional system of life prescribed the Prophet (Pbuh) by neglecting his ideal ways, conducts and morals in true sense of their meanings. They are integral parts of our Iman. If we stick to them, we can regain our faded glory.

Question: Voter lists prepared by the governmental agencies are used for canvassing and casting votes. But in Gujarat, it was used for identifying the Muslims to kill them. Many Muslims were put to death and those left behind, were not provided with any rescue and consolation. It is clear that the Muslims in India are not safe. What should they do?

Answer: One can easily understand the genuineness of your feelings and grief. But at the same time, you must have also seen true lovers of human beings. You must have also seen the justice-loving and true patriotic non-Muslims who condemned the gross act of animalism. They are the people constituting the real fort of India. They are the true in inheritors of Ram. As guided by the Qur'an, we should not lose hope because truth wins in the long run.

Question: I have been married for the last ten years and have three children. My wife has not been behaving well with me for eleven months. She has been taken in by someone else. Whenever I try to advise her to behave well, she says that she does not want to live with me. She threatens to commit suicide. In view of my children, I do not want to divorce her, what should I do?

Answer: If you are not able to solve the problems alone, you should try to get it resolved by some of your close relatives.

Question: During the lifetime of Prophet Muhammad (Pbuh), women bought from the marketplaces were called 'Launds'. People made love with them without entering into marriage with them. Is that practice permissible for a Muslim now-a-days as well?

Answer: The act of selling and buying people has no Islamic sanction. Needless to say, the Prophet Muhammad (Pbuh) encouraged people to free their male and female slaves. He told that this act would fetch them great reward of Allah. Now we do not have those conditions under which male and female slaves were accepted in the society. So, that practice no longer has any sanction.

Question: I belong to a Syed family. I know a Syed cannot be the recipient of zakat, charity and so on. Can a Syed eat anything served by a family which is the recipients of zakat and charity?

Answer: Of course, a descendent of a family tracing its lineage to the family of Prophet Muhammad (Pbuh) cannot be recipient of zakat and charity. But there is no problem in using the items served by those people who are the recipient of zakat and charity.

Question: Is it a sinful act to answer back someone's wishing Salam while eating food? Is there any special instruction regarding this in the Qur'an and Hadith?

Answer: There is no clear instruction in the Qur'an and Hadith as such. But it is improper to talk to some one with one's mouth full of food. So, it does not seem proper to answer back some one's greeting before swallowing the morsel of food in month.

Question: The Muslims belonging to the areas torn by communal riots were kept in camps in a dilapitated state. Not to speak of financial assistance, they were not rendered even human help. Volunteers of investigating agencies, journalists and peace loving people were not allowed access to the camps. Why were the Muslims treated with such cruelty? Why didn't the Muslims and secular organisation raise their voice against this discrimination?

Answer: You are right. The relief camps in Ahmadabad, Baroda, Godhra and Lunawada were in very poor conditions. Media and volunteers of different organisations criticised them. The Muslim organisations and the organisations of other religions also came forward to render help to them.

Question: The word 'Miyan' is used for 'husband' as well as for a Muslim. Why do the Muslims call Allah as 'Allah Miyan'?

Answer: Miyan symbolises respect. It does not imply any relations.

Question: There is a quarrel between a brother and a sister. They have a strained relationship. Will their five daily prayer, Hajj and other worshipful acts be accepted by Allah?

Answer: It is Allah who determines the rewards for five daily prayers, Hajj and other worshipful acts. But it is not permissible for a Muslim to be not on speaking terms with other Muslims, for more than three days. It is a sinful act to break the ties of relationship. At the same time, it is a source of great rewards to maintain the ties of kinship.

Question: There is a man. He wants to pay pilgrimage to the holy house of Allah. His grand daughters are marriageable. But they are not given into marriage because their father does not have sufficient money. The grand-father says that it is not his duty to marry them. Is it correct for him to think like this?

Answer: It is not the responsibility of the grand-father to get his grand children married. So, he can go to pay the pilgrimage to the holy house of Allah. But if a grand father spends money that he has amassed to meet the expenses of paying pilgrimage the holy house of Allah, on the marriage of his grand daughters, it will be a great gesture of kindness and sympathy. Allah is kind and loves kindness. He rewards every worshipful act according to the intention of the doer.

Question: What is the meaning of Milad? Now-a-days some people criticise those who organise Milad.

Answer: 'Milad' is an Arabic word. It means celebrating one's birthday. It is a matter of great sorrow that some people criticise this act as well. Prophet Muhammad (Pbuh) conducted himself with everybody very courteously, sympathetically and respectfully. Obviously, we need to adopt his exemplary conduct and behave well with everybody.

Question: In some communal riots, the rioters deflower the chastity of girls. If a Muslim girl commits suicide in order to avoid the assault on her chastity, will it be called suicide? Will she also receive the punishment meted out by Allah to those who kill themselves?

Answer: Suicide is an act of cowardice. It is permissible under no circumstances. One should be ready to face the challenges of life, even if one may lose one's life while grappling with those who are bent upon launching the attack. This is the reason that Islam accords great status to the martyrs.

Question: What is the meaning of Muzlum food? Are there any mentions of this food in Qur'an?

Answer: Islam prescribes for human beings the foods which are healthful. The food prescribed by Islam also includes meat of some permissible animals. At the same time, it prohibits the people from taking the meat of some animals. Obviously, the meat of the prohibited animals can be injurious to the health of the human beings. For example, chicken is allowed by Islam, so it is eaten after it is slaughtered in the name of Allah. But what you call 'muzlum', figures nowhere in Islamic books.

Question: If a male or a female Muslim passes away at a place where there is no Muslim, what shall be the manners of the performance of the last rituals? If he or she is buried after the performance of the rituals by the non-Muslims, will the deceased be meted out punishment?

Answer: After one's death, one is at the disposal of others. So, the deceased will not be responsible for his final rituals. Preferably, the people of the locality should look for some Muslims to perform the last rituals. In case there is no one available, then they can perform the last rituals with due honour they accord to any deceased. Allah knows everything that is why He does not punish anyone for others' deed.

Question: I had been involved in some gross deeds for several years. But I have brought myself to a sincere repentance. Will my repentance be accepted? Will my prayers be accepted?

Answer: Allah loves one's act of bringing oneself to a sincere repentance. To err is human. But if one seeks Allah's forgiveness sincerely, Allah forgives one. He says that those who regret and seek His forgiveness, are forgiven. You should regularly offer five daily prayers, feel repentant with due humility and sincerity. You should be optimistic of Allah's benevolence.

Question: What is Peer? What is the importance of 'Peerhood' in an Islamic society?

Answer: The word 'Peer' means an elderly person. By extension, it stands for a spiritual and religious guide.

Question: What is the meaning of the expression 'Assalam Alaikum, Wa Alaikum Assalam and Khuda Hafiz?' People say that those who wish Salam are rewarded with more virtues than those who answer back the greeting. Is there any fixed percentage of rewards for greeting and greeting back? Is shaking hands a sinful act?

Answer: The expression 'Asalam Alaikum' means 'may you earn the blessings of Allah.' Similarly, the expression 'Khuda Hafiz' means 'may God protect you'. Those who wish Salam get more rewards than those who answer it back. But there is no fixed percentage. Allah's rewards depend on one's sincere intention and also on His kindness and mercy. Shaking hands warmly creates the bond of love and affection, as also strengthens the relationship.

Question: When a Muslim dies his relatives arrange for a gathering on the third day for the recitation of the verses of the Qur'an. It is termed as Fateha. Is it a correct practice in the light of Qur'an and Hadith?

Answer: There is no verse of the Qur'an and saying of the Prophet (Pbuh) making mention of Fateha on the third day. But it's a common practice among the Muslims to gather at the place of the deceased for the recitation of the verses of Qur'an so that the deceased can receive Allah's rewards and blessings in his or her grave. Some people also feed the poor with a view to earning reward of Allah on behalf of the deceased. Of course, it is a practice prevalent among non-Arabs. It may be the product of cultural influence among the Muslims in the subcontinent.

Question: I get angry at even petty things very easily. Sometimes, it is beyond control. This anger leads to some losses. Before some time, I used to lie down in order to mollify my anger. I used to cool down very easily but now-a-days my anger does not subside. It lingers for a long time. Can you prescribe me, some supplications which may help me suppress my anger?

Answer: One who gets angry should recite 'auzubillah…'. It means 'I take Allah's refuge from the accursed'. If one is in a standing position while in anger one had better sit down or lie down. One should also drink water. The act of suppressing one's anger has been highly appreciated in Islam. The meaning of one of the sayings of Prophet Muhammad (Pbuh) is that powerful is not one who defeats a powerful wrestler, but it is the one who suppresses one's anger. If these things do not work, one should take medical advice.

Question: I am a shopkeeper. I never pay income and sales taxes. Whenever the income tax officials come, I escape. Is the money earned from my shop lawful or not?

Answer: Money earned through honesty and the prescribed ways is lawful. You should not fear the income tax officials. If you find that your earning is within the taxable amount, you should pay the due tax in conformity with the rule of the law.

Question: Some anti-social elements launched an attack on Akshardham Mandir situated in Gujarat. They wanted to provoke communal riots. It was a hateful and condemnable act. But the Home Minister reached Gujarat and controlled everything well within time. Wasn't it possible for the government to take such a step to save thousands of innocent lives who were put to death in Gujarat?

Answer: The attack on Akshardham Mandir was vehemently criticised and condemned by the Muslim countries. A confirmed plotting against the Muslims, it really aimed to provoke communal riots. The promptness of the government is praiseworthy. If the government had shown the same promptness, the genocide in Gujarat would have been averted and it would not have slurred the reputation of India. But we should be hopeful of the government's positive steps. We should also hope that this kind of genocide will never be repeated in India.

Question: There are several sects in Islam: Hanafi, Hambali, Maliki, Shafai and so on. The Muslims are so much divided on certain issues of their beliefs that they nurse extreme feelings of dislike for one another. They do not enter into marriage with the persons belonging to other sects. Is it possible to assemble the scholars of all the sects in order to create a consensus among them? Isn't it possible to obliterate the differences of opinion or rather obliterate all the sects for the sake of unity, brotherhood and mutual co-operation? Don't you think that diversity of sects in Islam has led the people to believe that the fundamentals of Islam are weak? What are the possible solutions?

Answer: Differences of opinion and existence of several sects within Islam implies democratic values. Such differences of opinion are held to be good for the welfare of the Muslim community. In the Indian context, one may cite the example of Indian Constitution which is interpreted by judiciary and legal experts differently. One is free to choose the way one likes. It is against the spirit of Islam to fight over such issues.

Question: Every religion offers its peculiar interpretation of the reality of God, happenings of the universe and social cultures. Everybody's religion is the most reliable source for him. He thinks his religion is the only true religion. The fact is that all religions have failed to provide justifiable principles like those given by modern science. Moreover, the principles of no religion are universal. This is the reason that no religion has been able to win the unanimous favour of all the human beings. How will you solve the problem of one, who wants to know the reason?

Answer: I cannot give my opinion about the conflict between religion and modern science mentioned by you in the light of other religions. As regards Islam, I can say that there is no conflict between Islam and modern science. Science tells what this universe contains. But religion tells why these things exist. The Qur'an does not deny the scientific facts. We should also keep in mind that scientific findings are not absolute. They are liable to change. But the principles of a religion remain unchanged.

Question: The parents of a girl want her to leave her husband. But the husband's family doesn't want them to terminate the bond of marriage. Moreover, they also threaten to go to the court, in case the bride's family doesn't listen to them. Will the verdict given by Darul Qaza under such circumstances be deemed valid?

Answer: It is better for both the families to sit together and seek solutions of the problems. In case there is no possible solution, the decision given by Darul Qaza should be accepted. One cannot predict whether the court will agree with Darul Qaza's verdict or not.

Question: After the riot in Gujarat, the (then) Prime Minister of India visited Gujarat. He had to fight back tears to see the cruelties perpetrated on the people of Gujarat. He said that it was the most ruthless and dreadful riot after the independence of India. During his speech in New York, he had said that riots like the one in Gujarat were common in India. Isn't it against the Muslims? I think such things encourage and inflame the riots?

Answer: I agree with your opinion. Politicians are in the habit of giving statements as the party line and the situation demand. In fact, several Hindus including many intellectuals, journalists, social workers and jurists blamed the centre as well as the state government for the gross act of communalism.

Question: I am a 28 years old girl. I have done B.A. I am in love with a Christian male aged 30. I have accepted him as my husband. He loves me very much and takes care of me. He is a government employee. Does Islam allow me to marry him? Will some Qazi perform the rituals of our Nikah?

Answer: According to Islamic laws, both bride and bridegroom are required to accept Islam as their religion before the performance of the rituals of Nikah. Obviously, you and your lover want to enter into marriage through the ways prescribed by Islam. So, he is also required to affirm his faith in Islam. I believe your parents will accept my suggestions. You should try to win the favour of your parents and inform your lover of the fact. You are a girl with belief in Allah and His teachings.

Question: After the birth of a child, Azan is sounded into his or her ears. Can a lady also sound Azan into a child's ears?

Answer: It is a male member of the family who sounds Azan and Iqamat into the ears of the newly born baby. In the absence of a male member of the family, a lady can also perform this act.

Question: There are several sects known as Islameeli, Dawoodi and Bohra. Are they considered as Islamic sects?

Answer: These sects that claim to be Muslims and have been accepted as Muslims by the common Muslims are Muslims.

Question: There are certain Muslims who go from door to door for the sake of raising 'chanda' (fund) for mosques and madarsas. They also take certain percentage from the income. Is this income lawful? Is it permissible for one to give one's money to such a person? It is believed that non-payment of zakat leads to drought. Is it so?

Answer: Those people who travel from one place to another for raising the funds for mosques and madrasas devote their time. If they take a proper percentage from the income, there is nothing bad in it. The non-payment of zakat has nothing to do with the state of rainlessness and drought. But sometimes, the disobedience to the Islamic laws leads to social trouble, affecting many people.

Question: Now-a-days the Muslims do not follow the lawful prescribed ways at the time of the division of their property. For example, everyone grabs the property, under his possession. Is this a correct prescribed way of division?

Answer: No, it is not in consonance with the Islamic laws. There is a complete system of division of properties and every member of the family has his or her fixed share in it. It is wrong to deny anyone his or her right to property.

Question: There is a man. He wants to usurp the property of his brother. On the demand of the division of property, he asks his brothers to accept Rs. 50,000 each. He pressurises them to give their property for Rs. 50,000 only. He says that this is the gift that he can give to them. He is intending to pay the pilgrimage to the holy house of Allah. Will his Hajj be accepted by Allah?

Answer: If what you said is correct, he will not be forgiven by Allah.

Question: Tell me the name of a book in Hindi, through which I can gain some knowledge about Islam.

Answer: You can study books, namely, 'Islam Praveshika', 'Islam Ek Nazar Mein', 'Islam Kya Hai' and so on.

Question: Is it a sinful act for a Muslim to deal in crackers and colours used on the occasion of Holi?

Answer: It is lawful to deal in every commodity which is not injurious to human health and society.

Question: Is it permissible for a male to apply henna and wear silk clothes? Is it permissible for a woman to go out without the permission of her husband?

Answer: Males are allowed to apply henna on their head and beard. They are also allowed to wear silver rings on their fingers but it is not proper for them to wear silk clothes. According to Islamic laws, a woman had better not to go out of the house without her husband's permission unless there is some emergency.

Question: Can two adult real sisters enter into marriage with the same male? If two adult girls are not real sisters, can they enter into marriage with the same male?

Answer: According to the Islamic laws, no male is allowed to marry two real sisters at a time. It is forbidden (haram). The Qur'an explicitly mentions the persons with whom one cannot lawfully enter into marriage at a time. If two adult girls are not real sisters, one can marry them at a time. In other words, one can enter into marriage with those who are not forbidden by the Islamic laws.

Question: Who will be the 'Wali' on the occasion of the marriage of a girl and a boy, if their parents are not alive or not present over there?

Answer: One's grandfather, greatgrand father, brother of grandfather or their children or uncles or their children can become the 'Wali'. According to Islamic laws, the bridegroom can himself be his Wali. If a widow has her father or elder son, he can be a Wali on her behalf.

Question: I want to marry the daughter of my father's sister. Some people say that marriage between close cousins lead to complications. What is your opinion?

Answer: If the members of your family are ready, you should marry her. As regards physical complications in the next generation, one can overcome them with the helpful diet, medical attention and proper education and training.

Question: What is the meaning of Mehr? How is it paid?

Answer: It is an amount fixed at the time of Nikah. According to Islamic Sharia, one has to pay the amount before touching one's wife. The wife should be made the owner of the amount.

Question: What are the reasons of exhibitionism and immodesty among the Muslims? Is it due to carelessness of the parents, guardians or due to the exposure to nudity propagated by T.V. and cinema? Indonesian Muslim women raised their voice against nudity but the Indian Muslim women follow the western culture. What is your opinion?

Answer: Islam prescribes the most ideal ways for one to live one's life in an ideal society. But some people fail to strictly follow the laws. This is the reason of aberration and straying away from the right path. But our close scrutiny reveals the fact that most of the Muslims live within the bounds prescribed by Islam.

Question: Suppose a girl is in love with a boy and is the family way without entering into marriage with him. Are they permitted to enter into marriage?

Answer: Yes, they can enter into marriage. The Qur'an explicitly says that an adulterer will marry an adulteress.

Question: The cat is included in the list of the animals whose meat is prohibited by Islam. But it is normally seen that people use the food items from which a cat has taken a few bites. Why is it so?

Answer: Since the cat is a domestic animal, it is difficult for one to ensure that she does not touch the eatables. This is the reason that we are permitted to use the left over of a cat. If one does not like, one is not forced to eat it.

Question: Does Islam believe in casteism? Is it permissible for one to use caste as a title?

Answer: Islam regards all human being to be equal because they have descended from Adam and Hawwa. According to a saying of the Prophet (Pbuh), neither Arab has any preference over any non-Arab, nor a non-Arab has any superiority over an Arab, also a white has no superiority on a black nor does a black have any superiority over a white. But it is not against Islam to use one's family title for the sake of identity. But no one is petty or great in the sight of Allah, except by way of piety and good deeds.

Question: What is Muta? What is the difference between Muta and Nikah?

Answer: Muta refers to the period of time agreed by a male and a female entering into marriage. On the contrary, Nikah is not for a fixed period of time. The bride and the bridegroom enter into Nikah with an intention to stay together as life partners as long as they live. According to the Islamic Sharia, followed by Ahle Sunnat, Muta is strictly forbidden.

Question: How many sects are there in Islam? Is there any sect that does not follow any Imam?

Answer: Sunni Muslims follow four Imams, Imam Abu Haneefah, Imam Malik, Imam Shafaee and Imam Hambal. The people belonging to yet another school of thought known as Ahle Hadith follow no Imam. There are sub-sects among the followers of four Imams as well as among Ahle Hadith. Similarly, Shia Muslims also have several sub-sects besides Imam Jafar's followers.

Question: I have a friend. He was in the habit of making thefts. But he has abandoned that bad habit now and has started working as an assistant at a shop. But he still has some stolen items with him. He does not want to use them. What should he do with those goods?

Answer: The resolve of your friend to abandon his habit of stealing is laudable. He should give the items stolen back to the real owners. If he does not remember as to whom the stolen goods belong or there is no trace of the real owners, he may distribute them among the poor with an intention to earn Allah's pleasure. In addition, he should sincerely seek Allah's forgiveness.

Question: There are several sects in Islam. There is acrimony of disputes, between Shias and Sunnis. I think the scholars of both the sects should sit together in order to end the conflict through mutual understanding. What is your opinion?

Answer: I agree with you. Islam lays a great emphasis on the unity, brotherhood, amity and harmony.

Question: I am a young Muslim. I am in love with a girl belonging to another caste. Can I marry her against the wishes of the members of my family? Is there any option other than court marriage?

Answer: Islam allows no casteism. As regards court marriage, Islam allows every adult Muslim male and female to marry according to their own choice. Marriage is not only a way of uniting a male and female but also a social contract. You had better enter into marriage with the blessings of your elders.

Question: Why does not Milli Council establish schools and colleges everywhere in India? Jamat-e-Islami pools money by gathering the skins of animals slaughtered on the occasion of Idul Azha. Why doesn't it establish hospitals for the poor everywhere in the country? Do its objectives include only one thing - becoming active during different general elections in the country?

Answer: Milli Council and Jamat-e-Islami are active everywhere in their own ways. They are contributing their share towards education and health. You had better made these organisations aware of your expectations from them.

Question: Some women visit the graves of different saints. They burn incense sticks and camphor over there. Do these acts have the religious sanction?

Answer: The Islamic scholars belonging to every sect – Deobandi, Barelvi, Ahle Hadith and so on unanimously agree that women should not visit the graves or mausoleums of the saints. There are only a few people associated with the mausoleums who say that the women have religious sanction to visit the mausoleums. But some of them do not allow them to go near the grave.

Question: My wife never obeyed me. Much to my chagrin, she disobeyed me openly. With a lawyer and a witness, I divorced her on 31st of July, 2000 through telephone. I also got it published in newspapers on August 9, 2000. When she came to my home, I pronounced the word 'talaq' in front of her. Then, I sought a Fatwa from Mufti Shah Abdul Qayyum (Aligarh). I entered into a new marriage. Was talaq valid or not?

Answer: There is no scope to say anything after the verdict given by Mufti Shah Abdul Qayyum. It is correct and acceptable.

Question: A woman can undertake the journey to Makkah for the performance of Hajj with her husband, father or brother. Can you name other relations with whom she can undertake the journey to Makkah for the performance of Hajj?

Answer: She can undertake the journey to Makkah in order to perform Hajj with all those who are mahram. The term 'mahram' in Islamic terminology refers to those relations with whom she can not lawfully enter into marriage.

Question: Tell me something about a caste known as Malik among the Muslims. Can they marry in Sayyed families?

Answer: Islam permits no division on the basis of caste system. I do not know with which so-called category of caste Malik families are identified.

Question: Who is responsible for sectarianism in Islam, common people or the scholars of Islam? To my mind, scholars of Islam are more responsible for sectarianism. I have a good example of it. There are two or three well established madarsas in my town. Two of them belong to Deobandi sect and one to the sect known as Barelvi. The students studying in Deobandi madarsa develop Deobandi thoughts, and those who study in Barelvi madarsa develop the beliefs held by Barelvis. They preach Islam according to their specific beliefs. What is your opinion?

Answer: I think a good scholar of Islam does not divide the community in the name of sects and castes. Since he is a true heir of the Prophet (Pbuh), he forges a bond of relationship between people. The act of creating conflict and making people fight among them does not behove the scholars of Islam. As regards the differences of opinion among different sects, the fundamental beliefs of all the sects are the same and the madrasas have been created for the propagation of these fundamental beliefs. The basis of differences of opinion lies in the interpretation not in fundamental beliefs.

Question: If all Dalits embrace the faith propagated by Islam, the destructive Brahmin system can be uprooted from the society. It will lend the Muslims social power and will also lead to religious balance. People will not dare to repeat the history of Gujarat anywhere. What is your opinion?

Answer: Islam has been practised in India for eight centuries. But the Brahmin system of society has been existing for thousands of years. Several attempts had been made by Dalits to resolve the problems existing in the society. Many Dalits embraced the faith propagated by Buddhism under the leadership of people like Baba Saheb Ambedkar, as also under the leadership of Udit Raj in the recent past. But there is no palpable change in the society. It is crystal clear that our call for social equality and justice can be materialised only through democratic and secular spirit. We need to be true to our democratic and secular ideals. We should also learn to accord respect and reverence to other religions and disseminate our active philosophy that is; live and let others live. Last but not the least, one's conversion to other faith is strictly a personal affair, based on free thoughts and inner voice.

3
Political Questions

Question: Mr. Asad Madani, former President, Jamiat Ulma-e-Hind had initiated a movement to safeguard the community and the nation. What were its objectives?

Answer: Its objectives included sincere attempts to fight against the communal forces, to condemn the failure of the government, to curb the riots and also to raise concerns for the beneficial and protective causes of the Muslims and the Dalits.

Question: When was the Jamiat Ulma-e-Hind established? Mention the names of its important leaders.

Answer: Jamiat Ulma-e-Hind was established in 1919. Among the important leaders of the organisation were: Shaikhul Islam, Maulana Hussain Ahmad Madani, Mufti Kifayatullah, Maulana Ahmad Sayeed, Maulana Hifzur Rahman, Mufti Atiqur Rahman Osmani and Maulana Syed Asad Madani.

Question: In the 27th Convention of the Jamiat Ulma-e-Hind, held in Ramlila Ground, Delhi, some years ago a proposal to form a separate political party for the Muslims was approved. Will it be beneficial to the cause of the Muslims? Or, will it further strengthen the forces working against the Muslims?

Answer: In the 27th Convention of Jamiat Ulma-e-Hind held in Ramlila Ground, Delhi, there was no call for the formation of any political party, rather a committee had been constituted to deal with the pros and cons of the formation of a separate political party for the cause of the Muslims. In this context, a clarification by the secretary, department of Media cell Jamiat Ulma-e-Hind, was circulated through a couple of news papers. As regards the question of formation of a separate political party for the Muslims, the Indian Constitution ensures this right to the Muslims. But we should always remember that there should be no space of self-proclaimed and self-styled functioning in the democratic and secular system. Therefore, it is essential to work jointly and collectively for the uplift of different group of the society and to uphold the democratic values and the structure of the country. There is a hatred and communal frenzy perpetuated constantly in the present days' atmosphere. Any such misconceived decision may consolidate and strengthen the anti-Muslim forces.

Question: What are Jamiat's objectives? Highlight the role of this organisation in the Indian National Movement.

Answer: The initial objectives of the formation of this organisation included sincere attempts to forge a bond of relationship among the scholars of Islam and help them to sit together and participate collectively in the independence movement and fight against the Britishers tooth and nail, as also to protect the general as well as religious cause of the Muslims. Jamiat Ulma-e-Hind right from the beginning, in principle, has got a distinction in promoting the Indian national integration as an integral part of its significant aims and objectives. This organisation was at the forefront against the two-nation theory approach initiated by the Muslim league for the partition of the country. This has to be understood that the people related to Jamiat Ulma-e-Hind happened to be the alumni of Darul Uloom Deoband, which represents a school of thought, against which heinous propaganda has been launched.

Question: What measures have been taken by the international Islamic conference for the communal harmony in India?

Answer: No country or International organisation can do anything with regard to the social well-being and communal harmony of another country. I think they had better not take any initiatives in this respect. These responsibilities should be undertaken by every patriotic and honest citizen of that country, as also by its social organisations and the government. No country can allow others to interfere in its internal matter, if it has a sense of pride in its nationalism.

Question: Is it possible in an Islamic state for a woman to become the head of the state? Is it permissible for the women in the Muslim society? Why have distinctive positions been offered to males alone? Why have females been deprived of everything?

Answer: If you make an in-depth study of the Qur'an and Hadith and that too with no prejudice and preoccupied notions, you will come to know that it is Islam alone which accords ultimate respect, dignity to and ensure several rights for the women. These important features of a society never existed before the advent of Islam. It is not possible for any sophisticated modern society to accord a status to women higher than the one accorded to them by Islam. As regards the question of a woman's becoming head of an Islamic state, there is no such prohibition in Islam. Maulana Ashraf Ali Thanwi, a renowned Muslim religious scholar of the 19th and 20th centuries, justified through a religious decree, the instance of a woman's becoming the head of the state in Bhopal. It is significant to mention that during this period, some women constantly became the head of the state. Pertinently, the number of women heads of the state or government in Muslim countries outnumber of women heads in any other country. Leaving alone Razia Sultana and Chand Bibi of the Medieval period, one can conveniently make mention of Benazir Bhutto becoming the Prime Minister of Pakistan twice, Sheikh Hasina and Begum Khaleda Zia in Bangladesh, Tansuchiler in Turkey, Megawati Sukarnoputri in Indonesia. They held highest offices as the leaders of their countries.

Question: Usually the Muslims happen to be the blind followers of unapproved and illogical religious things. They are meat-eaters and tyrant by nature and inculcate only religious education to their children. This is the reason that they are superstitious, self-centred, fundamentalist and orthodox. They adopt hero-worship for their leaders. They are the citizens of India but highly speak of Pakistan and Saudi Arabia. Do you agree with these things or not?

Answer: It does not mean that only non-vegetarians are tyrants and oppressors. If it had been so, the vegetarians would have hated disruptive activities and there would have been no communal violence in places like Gujarat, where thousands of people were massacred. A large number of non-vegetarians were butchered by the vegetarians. So far as the question of religious education is concerned, Islam is a religion which is firmly based on the philosophy of peaçe, fraternity, integrity and truth. If the religious education is disseminated in true spirit, the evils, like selfishness, hero-worship and wayward fundamentalism may be uprooted. It is not true that the Muslims, living in India support the cause of Pakistan and Saudi Arabia. I don't see any Indian Muslim who speaks highly of Pakistan. As far as the Arab countries are concerned, they have holy places of the Muslims, so they accord them respect and reverence. For that matter, people of every religion venerate their holy places. But their veneration of the holy places never conflicts with their patriotism. The

Hindus living in West Indies, Trinidad, Tobago, Fiji, Mauritius, Sri Lanka, America, Europe and South Asia venerate their holy places in Varanasi, Pryag, Haridwar and others. Similarly, for the Buddhists, Jains and Sikhs settled in different countries, visit, their religious places located in India, and these holy places will remain the source of attraction and veneration.

Question: Some VHP and RSS leader have been demanding change in some verses of the holy Qur'an for quite some time. Why aren't these people who are denouncing others' religion branded as terrorists? Will they dare seek such changes in their religious books? Such unwarranted activities cannot be tolerated by the community of Islam.

Answer: Those who are talking about introducing changes in the Qur'an are either ignorant or mere perpetrators of the communal frenzy. One should not get agitated by such statements. Moreover, it's only non-sensical to demand such things. Whosoever is involved in striking any type of terror is no less than an evil spirit. No religion supports such gross acts of ruthlessness.

Question: What should the Muslims do against the gross acts of injustice against them? They are unfairly identified with the terrorists. Why aren't the acts of terrorism perpetrated on the Muslims in Gujarat by the Hindus and their leaders branded as Hindu terrorism?

Answer: The Muslims should initiate a thoughtful and meaning dialogue with the sincere people of Hindu community for curbing the propaganda where people spit venom while talking about Islam and the Muslims. The growing schism and misunderstanding may be undone. We should not forget that the communal hatred cannot be repelled with the same kind of acts. We have to replace the evil with what is better. As regards the cruelties perpetrated in Gujarat, sincere Hindus of the country have reacted sharply and condemned it unanimously. We should not lose hope. The Indian society will always have sincere people who will stay sensitively alive to their surroundings, and condemn and fight against every type of gross animalism.

Question: Name the Muslims of India who devoted and sacrificed their lives, for the nation.

Answer: There is a long list of the Muslims who sacrificed their lives for the independence of the country. Those who made prominent contributions are: Sirajuddaula, Tipu Sultan, Bahadur Shah Zafar, Bakhat Khan, Hazrat Mahal, Maulana Muhammad Ali Jauhar, Bi Amma, Maulana

Hasrat Mohani and his wife, Maulana Mahmud Hasan, Shaikhul Islam Hussain Ahmad Madani, Ashfaqulla Khan. Brigadier Usman, Hawaldar Abdul Hameed and many stalwarts sacrificed their lives for free India. Several Muslims laid down their lives in Kargil war also.

Question: Neither Muslims nor their religion is safe in India. Even their institutions and worship houses are not safe. Despite such insecurity, they show strongs feeling of patriotism.

Answer: We should initiate a dialogue with the majority group of the country at both levels, individually and collectively so that all such misunderstandings can be warded off. People of every community equally participated in the independence movement and contributed their share towards the development of the country. We should not worry about political ups and downs.

Question: Was there any threat to the Muslims after Narender Modi becoming Chief Minister of Gujarat, for the third time? Everyday and everywhere new Hindu organisations were sprouting in this state. Did government know all these? If these were known to it, why doesn't the government take any action against them?

Answer: This was not surprising to know about Narender Modi's becoming Chief Minister of Gujarat for the third time. No doubt, there could be some fear among the Muslim community about Narender Modi's becoming Chief Minister again. But there was no need to be so, since they lived in a democratic country with legal institutions and conscious citizens. Sometimes, excessive pain becomes the potion. A few people among the Hindu community are aggressive for the satisfaction of their ego. They are vitiating the atmosphere. They are distributing spears and trishuls. They are spitting venom. Even now, such disruptive activities may cause a social disaster. The central and state governments should be alert and control these activities, otherwise this would be disastrous not only for a particular community but also for the whole nation.

Question: Does our country have such a weak security that there is always some aggression from Pakistan? It gives us extreme pain when we find that the terrorists from Pakistan attack our temples and Parliament, but our leaders simply shout threats in their speeches.

Answer: This is not the lapse of our security policy. Our unique geographical location is as such that, despite strict vigilance, infiltrators are successful. Our military and paramilitary forces are devoted. They try to stop the infiltrators and also sacrifice their life for the sake of stopping it.

Terrorists do not enter the country by giving prior intimation. A little more efforts in strengthening vigilance on the border can improve the situation of the country. This is objectionable, if any Muslim is being blamed for this. Muslims cannot involve themselves in plotting conspiracy against their nation.

Question: How can the issue of Kashmir be resolved? Who is responsible for this issue? What is the role of the Kashmiri Muslims?

Answer: The issue of Kashmir can be resolved in the light of Indian Constitution by sorting out the complaints of Kashmiri Muslims. Second partition of the country in the name of religion is never acceptable. This is what the common Muslims think. Kashmir issue and its complexity are attributed to the sick psychology of Pakistan. On the other hand, we are also accountable to some extent. The same Kashmiris opposed the Muslim League and declined to become part of Pakistan and sided with India in the war of 1948, 1965 and 1971. Now why have they distanced themselves from New Delhi? As far as Kashmiri Muslims are concerned, we should not ignore the fact that the number of Kashmiri Muslims, who were put to death by anti-India terrorists outnumber the deaths caused to these terrorists.

Question: Does America wants to eliminate the terrorism or does it want to aggravate it? Arab world is affected by the Israeli terrorists. Palestinians were slaughtered at the behest of America. America had committed aggression against 23 countries after the 2nd World War. Isn't it high handedness of America?

Answer: I do agree with your thinking. America always acts according to its national interest, on the contrary it preaches lessons of ethics. Due to this dual policy there is resentment among the Americans from New York to Los Angeles.

Question: Vishva Hindu Parishad organised a meeting in Delhi. What steps should be taken by the Muslim in this context? Isn't this a matter for the Muslims to worry?

Answer: Muslims need not do anything for it. If there is any danger from any Dharm Sansad, then that is to the Indian Parliament. In the present atmosphere, Muslim should act with tolerance and perseverance. We should not act in a manner that Vishva Hindu Parishad succeeds in flaring up hidden communal agenda.

Question: This is evident that BJP and Vishva Hindu Parishad are Hindutva based parties and they are also working against the Muslims' cause to some extent. Despite these, some Muslim leaders are affiliated with these organisations. Aren't they accountable for the cause of Muslims?

Answer: We are not aware that any Muslim leader has got affiliation with the Vishwa Hindu Parishad. However, this is a fact that some Muslims are affiliated with BJP. The Muslims affiliated to this party will tell whether they are accountable to community or to their party. In a democratic system, every body has got the right to express his or her views and also has the right to join any political party.

Question: Pakistani includes Allama Iqbal among the list of the architects of Pakistan. But, he wrote the most famous patriotic song *i.e.,* 'Sare Jahan Se Achcha Hindustan Hamara'. What is your comment?

Answer: Iqbal had died nine years before Pakistan came into existence. Therefore, one can't include him in the list of the makers of Pakistan. In his presidential address, Iqbal had talked about the constitution of Muslim dominated states in the Indian Union rather he had not opined of anything like separate Muslim nation, in All India Muslim League summit held in Allahabad in 1930. Hence, talking about Iqbal in such a notorious tune is nothing but spreading the message of misconception about him. One could say anything against him, if he had lived till the formation of Pakistan, he could have said anything about its creation or could keep silence about it. Needless to say, its formation had caused heart-rending incidents. In general, this is a common habit of Pakistanis that they consider Muhammad bin Qasim, Sheikh Ahmad Sirhindi, Shah Waliullah, Tipu Sultan and Sir Syed Ahmad Khan as makers of Pakistan.

Question: I belong to a Hindu family. When India is looked down in Pakistan, the Muslims of Indian origin are of the opinion that betrayal with the nation is betraying one's own mother. They also say that Islam will be annihilated. They will no longer remain Muslims. There are some disruptive Hindu organisations like RSS and Vishva Hindu Parishad, who ask Muslims to join the mainstream. They also brand the Muslims as traitors. Sometimes, Pakistanis too brand Indian Muslims as traitors. The language of Pakistani people and the Indian fundamentalists is the same. Sometimes, I suspect whether they have the illegal relation with the Pakistani people. What is your opinion?

Answer: I completely agree with your statements. We are aware of these facts. But it is important for them to understand who unnecessarily create the atmosphere of hatred against the Muslims to please the dirty political thinkings of Pakistan. They say that Muslims and the followers of other religions are not safe in India. In fact, if Hindus and Muslims with the followers of some other religions can live with amity and peace, the concept of two nation-theory becomes meaningless. This was the basis which led to the creation of Pakistan.

Question: The issue of Kashmir has been unresolved since for over seventy years. The leaders are serving their own political interests. Indian government has been spending billions of rupees for restoration of peace but there hasn't been any proper solution. One lakh twenty thousand Indian Muslims pray for the resolution of Kashmir issue and for peace and prosperity in India, in the holy premises of Kaba every year. But the prayer is not granted. What is your opinion?

Answer: One cannot resolve issues and problems only through prayers and supplications. They become effective only when we practically and seriously put efforts into resolve the issues. Let us hope there will be a development of positive atmosphere in Kashmir.

Question: America is ahead in high-handedness. But no country dares raise voice against it. Today, America and its allies are openly terrorising and plundering Muslims of Palestine. This can be disastrous for the Islamic world. What could be its remedy?

Answer: If you read newspaper regularly and watch television for the news, you will be aware that there had been a growing resentment all over the world against American policy pertaining to Iraq. America itself never witnessed such a large internal protest as had been continuing against its campaign of Iraq war. Everybody including Hollywood film industry people, the labourers in New York had been registering protest against it. Two American diplomats had tendered their resignations against anti-Iraq policy of the Bush. Tony Blair, the (then) Prime Minister of Britain, had not only faced ire of both houses of Parliament but also of two hundred members of Labour party. The people of Iraq and Palestine are so badly inflicted with sufferings and ruination that it is not only harmful to the Islamic world but also to international peace and harmony.

Question: An organisation of Dalits and Muslims "Rashtriya Juta Brigade" talk about the unity of Dalits and Muslims and it does not include upper caste Hindus in its organisation. Before and after achieving independence, nobody raised the slogan of Aurangzeb. Not even any Islamic scholar did so. But this organisation has raised the slogan of

Aurangzeb. This organisation had arranged a rally against Hindu terrorism at Meerut. Bhartiya Janta Party and RSS people had stoned at the rally on raising slogan of Aurangzeb and confronted with the people participating in the rally. Should the Muslims participate in such types of organisations? The members of this organisation have declared that they will convert to Islam. Would it give any advantages to the Muslims?

Answer: Islam never propagates the feelings of revenge and hatred. Hazrat Muhammad (Pbuh) taught us exemplary things. He inculcated in us the values of choosing those things for others that we choose for ourselves. In order to protest against inhuman and uncultured principles of people, we should not adopt the ways which are not in consonance with religion, culture and principled manners.

Question: There are some people who intend to eradicate human values from the world. We are not unaware of them. Aren't the contractors of religion, including you, are not accountable for this? What would be your answer in life to come? Let me know your answer so that I too can get rid of sin.

Answer: I do believe that a few institutions, government and media are trying to create a foul atmosphere against Islam and Muslims all over the world. Due to these things, large sections of the people of the world are affected by irrelevant propaganda and the situation is getting worse owing to non-availability of truth about the correct principles of Islam and Muslims. There is a need of sincere and constructive dialogue to overcome the persisting confusion. Who do you think are the contractors of religion? You will be aware of this. As regards me, it is a false accusation against me. I do not hold myself to be the contractor of my religion. Islam has no scope of monopoly. The questions asked by people and the sincere and humble attempts of mine to answer them bear witness to my aims of dispelling wrong concepts about Islam, Muslims and their approaches towards the world.

Question: When was the Jamat-e-Islami established? Who was the founder? There are two units, one in India and the other in Pakistan. Does only one man lead both units of Jamat-e-Islami? Can you name those who head it?

Answer: Jamat-e-Islami was founded by Syed Abul Ala Maududi in 1941 at Darussalam in Pathankot. Jamat-e-Islami was also divided after the partition of the country. Initially, it was headed by Maulana Maududi and later by Maulana Tufail Ahmad at Pakistan. Now it is headed by Qazi

Hussain Ahmad. In India, Jamat-e-Islami was headed by Maulana Abul Lais and Maulana Muhammad Yusuf and Maulana Sirajul Hasan. Now it is headed by Maulana Jalaluddin Umri.

Question: What did the peace-loving countries do after the recurring trends of militancy and animalism in the American forces in Iraq? What was expected from then?

Answer: The demolition of Iraq by America and its allied forces was not only a matter of concern but also there was more a fear of growing injustice. Now for the protection of safety, security and integrity of the government of any country, a non-aligned movement is needed to be launched. Such movement should be given a new dimension at the international arena so that check and balance of power can be maintained and global peace can be restored.

Question: Mention the reason why even after strong protests were made in America, Europe, Australia, Russia, India and South Korea against the American attack on Iraq, the Muslim countries especially gulf countries made no such protests.

Answer: This is not true that there was no protest in the Muslim countries. There were massive protests in Malaysia, Indonesia, Bangladesh, Egypt, Iran and Pakistan. It is true that there were no protests in the gulf countries. It was due to the political system and the pro-American policies of the rulers of these countries. Secondly, there is no role of the citizens of these countries in the governments and their plannings, except by way of obeying the governments, submissively.

Question: The reasons for which SIMI was banned were not applied to other organisations. Why it is so? After, Ashok Singhal, Togadia, Giri Raj Kishore and Aditya Nath keep on spitting venom and spreading hatred through hate speeches, why aren't bans imposed on them under POTA?

Answer: An authentic answer to your question can be given by the Government alone. So far as my view is concerned, I believe we should deal severely with those people who are involved in flaring disruptive activities and causing damage to the nation and its people. The confrontation and wrong notions against each other can be removed by it.

Question: The role of Media during Iraq war was lopsided. It spread hatred against Saddam Hussain. Do the media—except Al-Jazeera—of the entire world have become the puppet of America?

Answer: The partial reporting of media regarding American attack on Iraq created such a bad atmosphere. But all media houses should not be blamed. Apart from Al Jazeera, Abu Dhabi Television and some other global media houses exposed the bohemian animalism and ruthlessness of American and British soldiers. They had wreaked havoc on the innocent people and their properties.

Question: Muslims have objection to adopt the Uniform Civil Code. India is a country for all its citizens, hence no one should be above Constitution. What do you think?

Answer: What will the advantages be of the implementation of uniform Civil Code? What would be the source of uniform civil code? Will it be of same pattern as implemented in the western countries or will it be constituted in consonance with the laws of different religions? This is evident that none of the Indian religious groups will accept western model of uniform civil code by replacing their religious laws. A uniform civil code made in consonance with different religious faiths, traditions, customs and religions will be a laughing stock. Will people agree to marry according to Christians, divorce as per the laws of Islam and distribute property among their children according to the Hindu faith? And if it is based on any particular religious faith, customs, traditions and culture, then people of other religious communities will not accept it. Therefore, it would vitiate the freedom of religion which is an integral part of the Indian Constitution.

Question: Cow-slaughter is considered as a sin as per the Indian traditions. But Muslims are not in favour of a ban. Can't the Muslims make some sacrifice for the cause of Hindu brothers?

Answer: I am shocked to know that you do not know the truth. The Muslims have never been against the law against cow-slaughter. If you go through the history, you will certainly come to know that Sir Syed Ahmad Khan, Muhammad Abdul Bari Firangi Mahali and many more Muslim Ulama had openly supported the prohibition of cow-slaughter. If any consensus was not made after the partition in this matter, it should not be considered that there was no protest on behalf of the Muslims. There was a protest from the Chief Minister of West Bengal Dr. D.C. Roy and non-Muslims from Kerala and north-east region against the ban on cow-slaughter. So, no consensus was possible. It is already banned in Utter Pradesh. This is also an interesting fact to know that in Kashmir, a

Muslim dominated state, people do not eat even buffalo meat, let alone cow meat. They eat goat and sheep meat.

Question: Why don't the Muslims get benefit of reservation in the government jobs?

Answer: It is not known to me whether there is any reservation for the Muslims in the government jobs. A couple of Muslim castes were included during the implementation of Mandal Commission. Those Muslims, who got jobs on the basis of their castes, should help others and the activists should also try their best to help others get jobs as per the reservation policy.

Question: America has waged biological, chemical and nuclear war to eradicate the gulf countries. Why hasn't it included Israel? Israel has never negated the existence of such dreaded weapons, whereas all Islamic countries of the gulf neither have capability to possess such dreaded weapons nor they have disagreed to conduct the inspection of their arsenals. Why only Muslim countries are being targeted?

Answer: You have raised a very important question. It has been nagging the entire world. The truth is that the American policy, concerning west Asia has two objectives: the attainment of the objectives set by America and safety of Israel. So, barring Israel, America keeps on targeting some or the other country at one or the other pretext.

Question: Should India support any government formed with the assistance of American interference?

Answer: When and how the government of India accepts the government of some other country, depends on the regional situations. The national interest of India also plays an important role at this juncture. Indian foreign policy is quite meticulous and well thought of.

Question: Isn't the UN a mere puppet of America? Hasn't it been proved by the attack launched by America and its allies on Iraq?

Answer: One feels inclined to agree that the UN had become a helpless and mute spectator on this whole issue. However, UN, its security council and its (then) secretary general Mr. Kofi Annan did not ratify the proposal of American attack on Iraq. For that matter its role should be lauded. Therefore, it is evident to the whole world that America and its allies could monopolise on the basis of the possession of huge resources and wield enormous power.

Question: Arab League and the Organisation of Islamic Countries have been unsuccessful in resolving the issues of Afghanistan and Iraq. In spite of the flop show of these two organisations, does the Muslim world expect anything more or should it go for the constitution of another organisation?

Answer: Immediately after the inception of OIC, its ineffective policy was exposed to the world. In fact OIC has never been the representative organisation of the Muslim world. India, the second largest Muslim populated country of the world, does not have any role in this organisation. Usually, Arab nation and Pakistan have used it for their ends. It has always disappointed people on every delicate situation. But Arab League has played a very effective role. No doubt, there is some weakness in it which one can easily sense. But it is a commendable that the jobs accomplished by the Arab League in adopting a resolution and ratifying in a conference held in Cairo regarding American attack on Iraq. In the present days, the rulers, happen to be the sole authority in these countries. So, if the present system is not reformed, then there is no in meaning constituting any such organisations.

Question: Praveen Togadia, a leader of Vishva Hindu Parishad, has openly accepted that they demolished Babri Masjid and flared the communal violence in Gujarat, as per the report of "Hans", a Hindi magazine. Seven or eight thousand Muslims were killed in the Gujarat communal violence. Didn't such violence come under the acts of terrorism and conspiracy against the country? Why did not government impose POTA on such people with a lot of hatred for other communities?

Answer: You have raised the question about the statement of those people who are involved in propagation of communal hatred. It is very important. If the government does not try to curb such heinous trends, it would be certainly disastrous for the country. This is known to you that some sensitive and loyal citizens like Kuldeep Nayar and Teesta Setalvad have filed a writ with authentic evidences. They have appealed to the court for strict actions against these people.

Question: Hazrat Muhammad (Pbuh) instructed the Muslims to counter the prevalence of cruelties. Americans attacked Iraq and caused ruthless destruction and perpetrated cruelties against the innocent people. But no Muslim country helped Iraq. Isn't it a disobedience to Allah?

Answer: You have blamed Muslim countries for not taking any action against American soldiers attacking Iraq. Perhaps you have forgotten the fact that Muslim countries do not have power. Most of them depend on America for the protection of their governments. So, such expectation from them is meaningless.

Question: The Muslims have already got All India Muslim Personal Law Board. Why have they also established Islamic Fiqh Academy? Maulana Mujahidul Islam Qasmi steered both organisations. Why were two organisations established for the resolution of issues of similar nature?

Answer: Muslim Personal Law Board was collectively established under special circumstances by all classes and groups of Muslims community in December 1977. The objective of the organisation was to fight against the amendments and abolition of Muslim Personal Law. It also aims at eradicating the evils spreading in the Muslim society. The objective of the establishment of Muslim Fiqh Academy was to initiate constructive dialogues in academic domain and develop a consensus among the Muslims in respect of Islamic fiqh and wordily affairs so that issues and new challenges facing the Muslims may be overcome. The Late Qazi Mujahidul Islam had a great role in the establishment of Fiqh Academy. He was also the founder member of All India Muslim Personal Law Board. Since the post of the President All India Muslim Personal Law Board was vacant due to the demise of Maulana Syed Abul Hasan Ali Nadvi, Qazi Mujahidul Islam was appointed the President. And after his demise, Maulana Rabe Nadvi has been elected the president of the board.

Question: Mr. Jamali, the (then) Prime Minister of Pakistan, had again commenced a series of dialogue with India government. Could such dialogue enable both countries to develop an atmosphere conducive to the bilateral relationship?

Answer: The series of dialogue were initiated by the Indian Prime Minister. According to the past experiences, we did not have too much expectation from such dialogues. But we needed to collectively pray for the evolution of the atmosphere conducive for the growth good relationship between these countries. It may help us to overcome the feelings of hatred and take sincere steps towards peaceful and friendly relations. Pakistan should understand that there is always a great scope of resolution of all issues with the help of bilateral exchange of views. War is itself a very painful and complex issue. It cannot be the solution to any issue. Let the talk for better relationship and establishment of peace continue.

Question: Under the leadership of Imam Khomeini, the Islamic revolution took place in 1979 in Iran. The revolution seems to have been losing its stranglehold for quite sometime. Is it true?

Answer: In the beginning of the Islamic revolution of Iran was quite a force to reckon with. But it gradually started losing its stranglehold, as every movement does with the passage of time. But the Iranian leaders and people are on their mettle and are continuously working for the consolidation and development of Iran and also to become a strong and well- fortified so that the way for the development of the country can be paved well. This is wrong to say that Iranians have distanced away from Islam. It is quite significant that the country is making successful experiments in the field of public governance, that too without transgressing the bounds set by Islam. The country ensures a large number of rights to all of its citizens belonging to different groups and castes. No Islamic countries have such precedents. It is significant to mention that Iran presents a beautiful example of Islam and modernisation.

Question: Shouldn't the Muslim play an important role in resolving the issues between India and Pakistan?

Answer: The initiative taken by various Prime Ministers does not signify the step taken on behalf of any particular community or castes. They are on behalf of every Indian. The Muslims also earnestly crave the establishing friendly relation with Pakistan, because such relations will further peace. It will let the two countries prosper.

Question: You have opposed the idea of separate political party of the Muslims. Since the Independence of the country Muslims have not been offered any key posts in any of the political parties of India, whereas Hindus, Sikhs and Christians have been given key posts in Congress Party. How long will the Muslim be considered as second grade people in the Indian politics?

Answer: I cannot ignore the truth. Of course, the state is pitiable. Still I am of the opinion that the Muslims should play an effective role in the political parties of India and also, fight for their rights. They should try to bring out the qualities of the people. The formation of individual political party will not be as fruitful as creating awareness among people to fight for their rights and grab them.

Question: Sir Syed Ahmad Khan had called the Indian National Congress a Hindu Party. What was the basis for that? Had the Muslim League been established only for that reason?

Answer: The reason behind opposing the establishment of All India Congress Party by Sir Syed Ahmad Khan was that he knew that the sentiments of Muslims were very easily roused. He had witnessed it during the revolt of 1857 against the British. The Muslims had played a very important role in it. Sir Syed Ahmad Khan was well aware of the fact that Muslims were quite backward in respect of modern education. They were lagging behind. But the Hindus were quite ahead. They had altered themselves and had embraced the modern learning. In fact, the congress was established by an Englishman, A.O. Hume. The purpose of establishing this organisation was neither to help the people get rid of the slavery of Englishmen, nor did it aim to start any public movement to achieve the desired goal. It is pertinent to mention that it was not only Sir Syed who alone disliked the formation of All India Congress Party but there were many contemporary Hindu brethren who were also sceptic about it. As far as the establishment of Muslim League is concerned, it was established in 1906 after the death of Sir Syed Ahmad Khan. Sos Sir Syed had nothing to do with all these. He had always been a supporter of Hindus and Muslims living together. He was one of the important stalwarts who promoted the existence of warm and meaningful cooperation between the Hindus and Muslims.

Question: BJP is a non-secular and anti-Muslim party. Its Manuwadi approach has been exposed. People know that it is a threat to the unity and integrity of the entire society and community. Should a Muslim support this party?

Answer: Every citizen of India has got rights under the democratic system. He can support any party. BJP has self-contradictory principles which hold many communities of the country quite non-seriously. Its ways are harmful not only for the Muslims but also for the country because they do not allow people to gather at the same platform and co-exist. Thus, the society will be the sufferer. The atmosphere of peace, co-operation and fraternity will not be promoted.

Question: On the death of Rajju Bhaiyya, the former head of RSS, even Prime Minister of India visited his house. Isn't it surprising? He headed the organisation which has been banned owing to its activities of spreading communal hatred. Will the PM of India go to the place of the head of Jamat-e-Islami Hind on his death?

Answer: We should not be guided by our ideologies in the matters of our social relations with people. Our relation should be so cordial even with our enemies that we can share their happiness and sorrows alike. As regards the presence of the Prime Minister or Deputy Prime Minister and other leaders on the demise of Rajju Bhaiya, one should not forget that all these people have alliance with RSS right from the beginning and they have never hesitated to brand themselves as Swayam Sevak. Therefore, no one should be surprised to see them attending the last rites of Rajju Bhaiyya. I would like to add that we should be armed with such qualities and so much tolerance that help to maintain our social ties even with our enemies especially on such occasions. Politics is merely a part of life. It should not affect our social life and ties otherwise the society will be vitiated.

Question: The statement of Lal Krishna Advani, the former Deputy Prime Minister, with regard to Babri Masjid-Ram Janam Bhumi dispute, that Masjid should not be constructed over there is interference in the matter of court. It is sub-judice. Don't you think that it is inept for a Deputy Prime Minister of India to make such statements?

Answer: It is really painful. Such statements should not be made. For last few years, situations have worsened. Now Constitution, democratic institutions and other secular institutions of India are not safe.

Question: On the one hand, it is said that there is equality in Islam and there is no space for caste and creed among the Muslims. Why does then, Muslim talk about reservation?

Answer: Of course, there is equality in Islam and there is no space for caste and creed in it. The people raise the issue of reservation not on the basis of Islam but on the basis of existing inequality in the Indian society. People talk about reservation because 22.5 per cent reservation is allotted to scheduled castes and schedules tribe and 27.5 per cent reservation is allotted to other backward castes as per Constitution. When there is a demand for the reservation to Brahmins, Thakurs and Jats, then why should it not be for the backward Muslims. Evidently, reservation is demanded on the basis of economic backwardness instead of religious faith.

Question: The followers of Islam claim that Islam can resolve all contemporary disputes. Despite that a country like Iran has virtually banished it. The reason is crystal clear that Islam is dead against the human wisdom. Islamic revolution proved to be a bubble of water. It made the life of Iranians quite miserable and they are lagging behind in every field. Everybody is well aware about the mishappenings in Iran. To what extent is it justifiable to blame CIA and MOSSAD for these?

Answer: I do not agree with the charges you have labelled against Iran. After the success of Islamic revolution, Islamic democracy came off with flying colours in Iran. It emerged with strength and zeal to open new chapters of Islamic democracy. It is marching ahead on the path of economic development. It is well known to the entire world. America and Israel have been openly opposing Iran, the world is aware of this as well. But this is also a fact that the relations between India and Iran have strengthened.

Question: There are many cases of atrocities in our country. We are merely silent spectators. We are unable to check them. Why is there such a chaos in the country? Why are Muslims branded as terrorists and Madrasas called the centres of terrorism? Why is not government taking any punitive action against those people? Ruthless killing of the Muslims in Gujarat, Godhra and Akshardham, and other bestial atrocities, how long will the Muslims keep silence?

Answer: In the present Indian society, there is an extreme level of atrocities. People are tortured, exploited and discriminated. Many communities of our society are struggling against these sordid affairs. In a democratic country, individualism has no meaning. One can solve the problems through mutual co-operation. This is the need of the hour that we should come close to each other by evolving a goodwill approach. When the present problem will transform into deep thought will, the deep meandering will lead to wisdom in the Indian society and the society will become a ground for our destinies to prosper.

Question: Vishwa Hindu Parishad, a fundamentalist organisation, wants to impose the uniform civil code. Judiciary also wants to do the same under the pressure. Isn't it an encroachment on Muslim, Sikh and Christian Personal Laws? Ours is a secular country. Why is secularism being abolished?

Answer: The issue of uniform civil code does not pertain to the minorities alone. It will adversely affect the large chunk of Hindu majority. Hence, this issue should not be seen as a problem of a particular religious community. Secondly, such beliefs and thoughts about Supreme Court are totally wrong. It does not act under the pressure of any particular political party. The Supreme Court has not delivered any judgement regarding uniform civil code. It was only a chief justice, who expressed his personal opinion.

Question: All opposition parties including Congress are calling POTA as an anti-Muslim act, whereas the act has been made against the terrorists, whether the terrorists group belonged to Hindu (ULFA), Sikh (Punjab), or Christian (North East). Aren't all parties branding Muslim community as terrorist?

Answer: The parties are raising voice against POTA. They are also pointing out the shortcomings. We do not consider POTA as an issue of the Muslim. But we neither ratify it as a correct step, nor do we consider it necessary. This is extremely painful for any well to do society. Let us remember that the TADA and MISA were misused to a great extent. We do believe that if the government is firm and determined, the existing laws are more than enough to teach the lessons to anti-social elements and run the administration successfully with an iron hand.

Question: Why are there occurrences of communal violence in Muslim areas only, even after 54 years of Independence?

Answer: It is deplorable that there is communal violence in the localities of Muslim minority even after 54 years of independence. The main reason for this is that there is mistrust between the majority and minority communities. They do not sit for the promotion of mutual confidence. Secondly, such elements are still there in the societies who are not able to forget the causes of the partition of the country. There is another cause of communal violence. The Muslims are getting economically sound day by day. Anti-social elements do not want them to prosper. Aligarh, Moradabad, Firozabad, Varanasi, Mumbai, Ahmedabad, Jalgaon, Bhiwandi and so on are the cities which one may name. The weakness of government machinery, and communal organisations and leaders, as well, is also responsible for such violence.

Question: Muslim voters always make use of their votes in favour of the parties that are supposed to defeat the BJP. What is the gain for Muslims?

Answer: If we look at the history of electoral process of the country, it is wrong to say that Muslims always use their votes to defeat BJP. When BJP worked as Bhartiya Jan Sangh, it had got massive support of the Muslims in the election of 1967, especially in the Muslim dominated localities. Anwar Ali Dehlavi, Muhammad Ismail and Begum Khurshida Kidwai were elected as members of metropolitan council from 1967 to 1989. They were all Jan Sangh candidates. They always fought from the Muslim dominated areas. Maulana Imdad Sabri became the Deputy Mayor of Delhi Municipal Corporation from Jama Masjid. He fought as a Jan Sangh candidate. This is a fact that success of Atal Bihari Vajpayee from the New Delhi parliamentary constituency in the parliamentary election of 1980, became possible only due to the support of the Muslim of Basti Hazrat Nizamuddin Auliya. Even in the election of 1989, a large chunk of Muslims supported BJP and Janata Dal candidates. For the last twelve years, BJP has replaced its political agenda and has adopted temple issue. It tried to create an atmosphere of fear due to which Muslims in the society moved to the peripheral areas and social and economic polarisation became effective on the ground of Hindutva agenda. Other political parties and leaders took advantage of these situations to gain dirty political mileage. In fact, Muslims always followed the right political track in the electoral process and showed the spirit of true nationalism and secularism. This is the reason that the Muslims never aligned with any Muslim political party. They are of the firm view that the politics of separation can never be beneficial for this country.

Question: Some of the people are of the opinion that Islam has been spread with the help of sword instead of its true and persuasive messages. Is it so? The Muslims of Arab countries are rich. Are the Muslims of other countries rich or poor? Do the Islamic banks accept interest?

Answer: This is a gross misconception that Islam spread with the help of sword. Had it been so, Muslims would not have been in minority despite seven hundred years of Muslim rule in India. All Muslim countries are not economically well off and rich. Muslims are both rich and poor like all other people belonging to other religions all over the world. As per my knowledge, Islamic Banks do not accept interest.

Question: Our country is like a body. The Muslims are also a part of that body. This fact is not digested by the fundamentalists who consider themselves as patriot. This is really a matter of great sorrow and the government is also silent over this issue. Aren't they cheating the nation? Do they deserve to be called leaders of the country? Aren't they leading the country to a disastrous future?

Answer: I do agree with your anxiety and concern. What can be done under such circumstances, if there are unruly people and worthless rulers? True nationalists keep silence and hypocrites and selfish people are professing themselves to be true nationalists.

Question: Why is India not made the member of O.I.C. it has one of the largest Muslim population in the world? Such a large Muslim populated country does not have any representation at the international level. Is there any concerted effort on behalf of any Muslim organisations or the government of India in this matter?

Answer: Yes, Organisation of Islamic Countries (OIC) is meaningless, as India does not have its representation in it because it has the second largest Muslim population in the world. India participated in its conference held at Rabat in 1969. But India was not included as a representative in the OIC because it is not an Islamic country, whereas there are still some countries which have got membership of the OIC but the Muslims in these countries are in minority. And they are not Islamic countries.

Question: There was a conference of OIC held in Khartoum, the capital of Sudan, on 30th June, 2002. Qatar proposed that India should be given the membership of OIC. But, organisation was of the opinion that if India was made a member, then Russia, U.S.A. and Israel would also have to be obliged as they have been demanding the same for a long time because Muslim population in these countries is sizable. What is your opinion about it? Isn't it dishonour for our country?

Answer: The reason why India was not given membership of the OIC is beyond comprehension. It is not plausible to reason to compare India with other countries. India has the second largest Muslim population in the world. If India is made the member of OIC, our secularism will surely be strengthened. It will harm it in no way. It is so because countries like Turkey, Indonesia and Malaysia believe in secular and democratic traditions, and they are the members of this organisation.

Question: The objective of the OIC is to restore peace by removing internal differences. Why hasn't it tried to resolve the differences between India and Pakistan?

Answer: This is a valid question. But the irony is that the country with the second largest Muslim population has not been given the membership in this organisation. Secondly, this is also a bitter truth that OIC did not have any prominent role in stopping the war between Iraq and Iran, conflict between Iraq and Kuwait, conflict between Iraq and Americans.

It also did not prove to be a proficient agency to scotch the rumours floated against Islam and the Muslims after 11th September.

Question: There are several roads and highways named after Gandhi, Nehru, Bose, Indira and Rajiv, whereas there is none named after Abdul Hameed Khan, Khan Abdul Ghaffar Khan, Abul Kalam Azad, Sir Syed, Husain Ahmad Madani. Didn't they contribute their share towards the independence of the country? Why is there step-motherly treatment with these patriots?

Answer: The roads and other structure named after great Muslims leader, freedom fighters and so on. Ajmal Khan park is named after Ajmal Khan, Khan Market after Dr. Khan Saheb, Kidwai Nagar and Rafi Marg after Rafi Ahmad Kidwai, Maulana Azad Road and Maulana Azad Medical College after Maulana Azad, Dr. Zakir Hussain Marg and Dr. Zakir Hussain College after Zakir Hussain, Maulana Muhammad Ali Marg after Maulana Muhammad Ali Jauhar, etc. Similarly, roads and other structures have been named after great Muslims in other cities as well, for example, Muhammad Ali Road in Mumbai and Aligarh. Now it is our duty to name the roads and build the memorials in the names of freedom fighters and architects of modern India with the help of municipal corporation or municipal board.

Question: According to you, no appeal from any mosque to vote and support a particular political party should be made. But the Imam of Shahi Jama Masjid Delhi has been making appeal to vote and support in favour or against a political party since 1977. What is your opinion?

Answer: We should not forget that the Shahi Imam of Jama Masjid, Delhi never issued such a decree. He expressed his opinion as a conscious citizen of India. This is his constitutional right Nobody can stop him from doing so just on the count of his being a Shahi Imam. Obviously, one's position is damaged, even if one makes some personal comments. In fact, he has never used the rostrum of Jama Masjid for this cause, at least to the best of my knowledge. Moreover, we should recall the period of emergency from 1975 to 1977. The oppressive regime was imposed under the garb of emergency and opposition leaders were imprisoned by demolishing the democratic traditions. In the face of cruelties perpetrated on the Muslims in Turkman gate area of Delhi, Khalapar of Muzaffar Nagar and in different areas of Mewat, Shahi Imam of Jama Masjid, Delhi, was courageous enough to have registered his protest. It was a laudable step. The leaders of Janata Party took his support to be a blessing and boon for themselves. Today a new issue has developed. Every individual claims to have the right to speak about religious matters. But religious leaders are not allowed to raise their concern and voice against oppression and injustice. Therefore, our stand is very clear that Masjid should not be allowed to be a platform of political propaganda. But equal opportunities should be given to the Imam to play an important role as a responsible citizen.

Question: Were opposition leaders in Legislative Assembly and Legislative Council of Uttar Pradesh (happened) Muslims before this as well?

Answer: As per my knowledge in the beginning of the sixth decade Abdul Jalil Faridi was the opposition leader of Legislative Council in Uttar Pradesh. He was affiliated with Praja Socialist Party. This was for the first time that in the Legislative Assembly and Legislative Council of Uttar Pradesh, the leaders of main opposition party were Muslims.

Question: It is said that Indian Constitution does not allow a Muslim to become the Prime Minister of India. Is it so?

Answer: It is a baseless rumour. Indian Constitution does not have any place for partiality.

Question: In our country, BJP is considered as a pro-Hindu party and Samajwadi Party is considered as pro-Muslim party. Actually these parties do not have any ideological differences. Both parties exploit religions to obtain personal gains. Neither BJP helps Hindu brothers in eking out a living nor does Samajwadi party extend any financial support to the Muslims. Do you agree with it?

Answer: I do agree with you. No political party works for the interests of the people of a religious group. If it does, it is purely for its personal interest, no matter, whether it is BJP or Samajwadi Party. That is why both Hindus and Muslims should work for their betterment. They should also work for the safety of democratic principles. They should nourish love and affection and further a sense of brotherhood and fraternity among them. They should not be taken in by any considerations. The healthy society can be built by virtue of the consolidation of social harmony and mutual love. Thus, people can co-exist. We should keep it in mind that short sightedness and differences always increase gulf and create unhealthy situations.

Question: Are all Mullas and Maulavis terrorists? Sangh Parivar burns their effigies. On the one hand, Sangh politicians brand Muslim as traitors, terrorists and dishonest people and on the other hand, they go to Dargahs for fulfilling their wishes. We are also from among them. Why do they bent on communalising the society of the country?

Answer: People are engaged in gaining their political mileage. They carry out their dangerous and hateful propagandas for serving their petty interests. Such people forget that they are not harming the Muslims, Dalits and Christians, but damaging the image of India on the whole. Shivji liked to become a Neel Kanth (bird) by taking poison in order to save the entire living creatures. Sadly, today some people are trying to inflame hatred and militancy by making an organisation in the name of Shivji. Bhaghwa colour, once the symbol of peace, sacrifice and sainthood for the welfare of people, is now unfortunately, used for attaining the mean political power. Obviously, oppression is bound to be scotched some day or the other.

Question: Our Prime Minister appealed to observe two minutes silence for the people, who lost their lives in the incident of 11th September. But no announcement was made by the P M to observe even two seconds silence when thousands of people were killed in the communal violence in Gujarat. Didn't the Prime Minister feel sorry for them?

Answer: Whatever was said by the Prime Minister of India at different places like Ahmedabad, Godhra and so on regarding the communal violence in Gujarat is known to all. It is quite heartening that many people and organisations of different types in different parts of the country registered their protests against the carnage of the Muslims in Gujarat.

Question: The national President of SIMI is of the opinion that he does not at all believe in the Constitution of India. On the other hand, Shahi Imam says that there is a war of independence going on in Kashmir. What would you like to say about both of them?

Answer: The President of SIMI did not give such a statement. So far as the statement of Shahi Imam is concerned, I do not know who attributed it to Shahi Imam. On Pervez Musharraf's visit to Delhi, Shahi Imam had candidly said to the leader of Hurriyat Conference Syed Ali Shah Gilani at home held at the residence of the Pakistan High Commissioner that Kashmir cannot be separated from India. He had added that whatever was going on over there, was not Jihad. He had also said the same thing in Jama masjid. The disruptive forces have threatened to kill him for this statement. If it is assumed for a moment that some people keep a negative attitude towards the Constitution of India, they should be countered with the positive and democratic approach and thoughts. These are the traits that differentiate democracy and autocracy.

4
Economic Questions

Question: Who are the deserving recipients of *Sadqa* and *Fitr*? Should the deserving recipients of *Sadqa* and *Fitr* also pay *Sadqa* and *Fitr*?

Answer: Those who are deserving recipients of *Zakat* are also the deserving recipients of *Sadqa* and *Fitr*. Those Muslims who do not possess alms-worthy wealth, but are somehow economically better can dispense charity. Those who are destitute and poor need not dispense *Sadqa* and *Fitr*.

Question: During one's life, one dispenses charity and terms it as '*Jaan ka Sadqa*' (charity for life). Can one also term the charity dispensed for a deceased as '*Jaan ka Sadqa*' (charity for life)?

Answer: Charity is dispensed for earning Allah's pleasure. The charity given on others' behalf aims at earning Allah's pleasure for them. It can be dispensed on behalf of the man who is alive, as also on behalf of those who are dead. The term '*Jaan ka Sadqa*' is an idiomatic expression.

Question: I borrowed some money from a money lender. It was agreed that I would pay the interest. I know that giving and taking interest is strictly forbidden in Islam. Now a Maulavi of my village says that I should not pay the interest. What should I do?

Answer: If someone has taken some money on interest from a money lender or from some Bank under some unavoidable circumstances, such as for starting one's business, he should return the money with due interest. The non-payment of interest may lead to prosecution. He may be meted out with some punishment as per the rule of the law. Those people who are against such practices must pool some money so that they can help out their needy brothers.

Question: I have a mango orchard. The crop was very good but the storm destroyed half of it. If I sell the mangoes, as per the market rate I have to bear a heavy loss. Can I sell them at a higher rate? Is the money earned through this way would be lawful or unlawful?

Answer: One can try to sell one's ware at any rate. It is upto the customers whether or not they buy it at that rate.

Question: I am a Central Government Gazetted Officer. I want to know the rules regarding interest. The answer should be in conformity with the conditions of India. I pay *zakat* every year. But I buy GPF, NPP and infrastructure bond for the curtailment of the tax levied on my earnings. I also earn some interest out of these bonds. Is it permissible to accept interest in view of the inflation rates? I keep my money in banks for the sake of security. I want to build a house. If I don't accept the interest, I would suffer a loss because the construction rate gets higher and higher every year.

Answer: There is a consensus among the scholars of Islam that the interest earned from banks does not amount to be reckoned as interest. As regards the essential deduction from your salary and retirement benefits, they are regarded as the lawful part of your salary.

Question: There is a person suffering from acute poverty. He has no one to bail him out. Can he take some money on interest for warding off his poverty? Is it forbidden (*haram*)?

Answer: Islam does not allow one to give or take interest. But, if one has no way out to save one's life, then one is allowed to eat even the carrion.

5
Educational Questions

Question: What type of education is imparted in Jamia Millia Islamia? Does it also impart religious education? If it imparts religious education, how is this education different from the one imparted in *madrasas*?

Answer: Jamia Millia Islamia, a product of our national movement, was established in 1920, in Aligarh during the Khilafat and Non-cooperation movements. It was shifted to Delhi in 1925. In 1988, it was accorded the status of a central University by an act of Parliament. It has several faculties. Islamiat, Hindu Ethics and Indian Religion and Culture are compulsory subjects for its school and undergraduate students. These subjects are taught with an objective to familiarise the Muslim as well as Hindu students with their religion. It is significant to mention here that the undergraduate students who have *madrasa* background have to study Indian Religions and Culture as a compulsory subject. Like any other University in India, Jamia Millia Islamia is a progressive university with the syllabi taught in most of the Indian universities.

Question: As it is evident from its name, Jamia Millia Islamia is a Muslim University. Does it have the provision for the Non-Muslim candidates to take admission?

Answer: You are mistaken. A central university, Jamia Millia Islamia University makes no distinction on the basis of caste, religion, region and language. Admission is granted on the basis of the percentage of marks obtained by the candidates in their admission tests. Noticeably, there are a few departments where Non-Muslim students are in majority.

Question: Tell me something about courses offered by the department of Islamic Studies in Jamia Millia Islamia.

Answer: Every undergraduate student has to study Islamiat or Indian Religion and Culture as a compulsory subject. Those undergraduate students who come from *madrasa* background have to study Indian Religion and Culture. Department of Islamic Studies offers B.A., M.A. and Ph.D programmes in Islamic Studies.

Question: I have passed intermediate and want to do B.A. in Islamic Studies but I know a little Urdu. Can I take admission in B.A. Islamic Studies? What are other subjects that I would have to study? Can a Hindu take admission to B. A. (Islamic Studies)?

Answer: In order to get admission to B.A. (Hons.) Islamic Studies you have to fill the admission form. The knowledge of Urdu is not essential. The medium of instruction and examination is Urdu, Hindi or English. Any one irrespective of caste, religion, or region can take admission to B. A. (Islamic Studies).

Question: I am studying in B.A. (1st Year). I have also done Adeeb, Adeeb Mahir and Adeeb Kamil from Jamia Urdu, Aligarh. Can I get admission to B.U.M.S. on the basis of Adeeb Kamil?

Answer: Contact the related office of Jamia Urdu, Aligarh.

Question: Nadwat-ul-Ulema (*College*), Lucknow is branded as the training centre terrorism. Now the students' union leader of the same college is subjected to oppression. The reason is that they don't support the fanatic and communal forces. What should be done?

Answer: Those who call such a prestigious educational institution the training centre for terrorism, are either ignorant or ill-intentioned. After the destabilisation of Talibani power in Afghanistan, the citizens of different countries fighting for Talibanis were caught over there. The Indian society must be proud of the fact that no Indian citizen was among them.

Question: Muslim youngsters are not interested in Urdu now-a-days. Does it show the meaninglessness and insignificance of the Urdu language?

Answer: It is not proper to make a sweeping remark, that too in context of the situations in India. The students study and speak Urdu in the regions where Urdu is the medium of instruction and examination. One may mention Maharashtra, Andhra Pradesh, Karanataka, Bihar and so on, as examples. In other words, the significance and importance of Urdu is still intact in these areas. Similarly, people study Urdu in Jammu and Kashmir and Himachal Pradesh. Even in Delhi students of various schools study Urdu and have Urdu as a medium of instruction and examination. Besides, the institutions of modern education, there are *madrasas,* where the medium of instruction and examination is Urdu. Of course, Urdu does not enjoy an important position at certain places due to the government's indifference and discouraging attitude. There is no doubt that Urdu is still the most prestigious and important language by virtue of the culture it represents and cerebral discussions one can have. But there is no denying of the fact that it does not have the potential means of ensuring its students' employment as some foreign languages do. This is the reason that the problem is aggravated. With the passage of time, Urdu has also lost the status it had once accorded to it. I would like to mention here that Urdu should not be considered as the language of the Muslims. Non-Muslims have also contributed a lot towards the invigoration of the canon of Urdu literature and language.

Question: I have done my intermediate and wish to pursue my career in Aeronautical Engineering. Tell me some institutions, where I can get admission.

Answer: I do not think there is any institution in Delhi offering courses in Aeronautical Engineering. Perhaps IIT, Kanpur offers this course. Contact the concerned department in IIT, Kanpur.

Question: How can we make the Muslim youngsters career conscious?

Answer: For over a decade, the Muslims have been taking more interest in education. They want their children and wards to pursue their career in education. As compared to other communities, we still lag behind. We need more well-concerted efforts to prepare the parents and guardians to attract them towards education. We have to highlight the bright prospects education holds. We also need to emphasise the fact that education helps one to have developed a personality. Needless to say, the development of personality helps one get a better job as well as compete and excel others in any field. In sum, we have to revolutionise the thought and attitude of people to attract them towards education.

Question: I belong to a economically weaker section. I am a student of class XII (Science). I want to become source cause of pride for my parents by virtue of my hard work and diligence. Tell me such a Muslim school that gives admission to students on the basis of their merit and also bears the expenditure.

Answer: One develops and sharpens one's intelligence and brilliance by virtue of hard work. And hard working students can come off with flying colours in any school. Two Presidents of India, Dr. Zakir Hussain and APJ Abdul Kalam, were the students of ordinary schools. But they achieved remarkable success by virtue of their hard labour and extraordinary brilliance. As regards scholarship, you should contact U.P. Waqf Board and some local institutions providing economic assistance to the disadvantaged.

Question: Shah Nama-e-Islam, a poetic work of Hafeez Jalandhari, is written in a highly exaggerated style. Is it proper to read it?

Answer: It is a poetic work narrating Islamic events. There is no harm in reading it. A poet employs different literary devices for the embellishment and beauty of his work. Of course, it is written in an exaggerated style. As regards one's affirming belief in something, one is required to affirm faith in the basic articles of Islamic beliefs.

Question: Does Islam allow one to have wealth and enjoy power? Islam teaches the believers to respect others' religions. But as reported by the press and electronic media, *madrasas* inculcate orthodoxy and dogmatism in their students. It is also said that no steps are taken to help the students to keep abreast of time. What is your opinion?

Answer: Islam does stop its followers from earning money for the sake of prosperity, and obtaining power and control. Wealth and power are not the indicators of luxury and extravagance. They are considered to be the means of dedicated service to human beings. As far as your second question is concerned, the Qur'an explicitly says that there is no compulsion in religion. If further asks the believers to declare, "I worship none whom you worship, none will you worship that will I worship." Furthermore, Islam strictly prohibits its believers to refrain from hurling abuse at others' objects of worship. The charge of fanaticism against the Muslims is non-sensical and baseless. Since the people who level the charges are not aware of the true spirit of Islam, they go on carrying out their false propaganda against Islam. It is incumbent on the Muslims to contact media persons and familiarise them with the true spirit of Islam. People should also be made aware of the objectives of *madrasas*. They bring up and educate destitute and disadvantaged children. As regards the modernisation of Madrasa Curriculum, it is important to note that *madrasas* are established with the objectives of imparting religious education. The so-called modernisation has no scope in Madarsa Curriculum. In view of the contemporary demands, Madrasas have also introduced some technical courses.

Question: Name the founders of Jamia Millia Islamia, New Delhi and Nadwatul Ulama, Lucknow. The graduates of Nadwatul Ulama are eligible for higher courses in several Indian Universities. Why are not the graduates of Darul Uloom Deoband eligible for higher courses in Indian Universities?

Answer: The foundation stone of Jamia Millia Islamia was laid by Shaikhul Hind Maulana Mahmood Hasan on 29th October, 1920. Its prominent founders were: Maulana Muhammad Ali Jauhar, Hakim Ajmal Khan, Dr. Mukhtar Ahmad Ansari, Maulana Azad and Dr. Zakir Hussain. Darul Uloom Nadwatul Ulama was established in 1895, in Lucknow. The most prominent name of its founder was Maulana Muhammad Ali Mungeri. Since the curriculum prescribed in Nadwatul Ulama includes English and other subjects of modern education, its graduates are eligible for admission to higher courses in Indian Universities. Moreover, its degree is recognised by different Indian Universities. On the other hand, the curriculum prescribed at Darul Uloom Deoband, primarily includes traditional religious subjects. The graduates of Darul Uloom Deoband are eligible only for higher courses like Arabic (Hons.) and Islamic Studies (Hons).

Question: I want to establish a Muslim minority school. Tell me how I can receive the grants from Maulana Azad Educational Foundation? What are the pre-requisites?

Answer: Maulana Azad Education Foundation functions under Ministry of Minority Affairs, Govt. of India. Minister of the concerned ministry is the head of this institution. The institution that intends to avail itself of the grants sanctioned by MAEF should be at least three years old. It should also have the recognition by the education department of the state. The plot of land for school building, hostel, laboratory, etc. should have proper registry. In sum, one needs to possess the basic infrastructure for applying for the grants. For further information, you can contact the Secretary Maulana Azad Education Foundation.

Question: I have my board exams this year. Can you prescribe some verses which I may recite as 'dua' and supplication for my success?

Answer: For success in exam one must study diligently. There is no substitute for hard labour. Combine your hard work with this dua, '*Rabbi Zidni Ilma*'.

Question: Name some reputed coaching centres for IAS and PCS exams where boarding and lodging are free and some stipend is also given.

Answer: Contact Director, Hamdard Study Circle, Tughlaqabad, New Delhi and Director, Coaching Centre, Jamia Millia Islamia, New Delhi.

Question: Tell me some government or non-government institutions offering correspondence courses. I want to learn the Urdu language.

Answer: Contact Director Arjun Singh Centre for Distance Education, Jamia Millia Islamia, New Delhi. The centre offers the courses in the Urdu language through bilingual approach.

Question: I am suffering imprisonment. I want to learn Urdu. It is pertinent to mention here, I learnt how to read the Qur'an in Jail itself. Tell me the easy way to read Urdu so that I may also be able to read books containing Hadith.

Answer: Contact Secretary, Urdu Academy, Kashmiri Gate, Delhi.

Question: I am 18 years old. I have passed Munshi from Arabic and Persian Board. Am I eligible to do intermediate? If I do Adeeb Kamil from Jamia Urdu, Aligarh, will I be eligible for Muallim from Jamia Urdu Aligarh? Can you name a modern course which is equivalent to Muallim?

Answer: Contact Arabic Persian Board, Allahabad, U.P.

Question: I did intermediate (Vocational). I have also passed the intermediate exam with Urdu as an additional Subject. I have done B.A. (Hindi and History) and Adeeb Kamil from Jamia Urdu Aligarh. I want to do M.A. in Urdu privately or through correspondence. Tell me a university in U.P. from where I can do M.A. (Urdu).

Answer: You may contact the Head, Department of Urdu, Choudhary Charan Singh University, Meerut.

Question: I am running a *madrasa* under a five year DPAP plan. I want it to run it afterwards as well. Tell me how to run it?

Answer: You should get it recognised by Arabic Persian Board of Uttar Pradesh.

Question: There are some orthodox leaders who believe that *madrasas* are the training centres for the terrorists, so they should be banned. Is there any way to check the leaders who have biased opinions?

Answer: It is a false accusation against *madrasas*. There is no denying the fact that followers of Al-Qaida, Osama bin Laden and Mulla Umar, nabbed in Afghanistan were not from India. Of course, H.R.D. Minister and Deputy P.M. made it clear that no *madrasa* was found involved in any anti- national activity. Now, if an individual or an organisation levels any false charge against *madrasas*, it is the duty of the Indian government to initiate appropriate action against them.

Question: I belong to a poor family. I did my B.A. by giving private tuitions. I want to be an I.A.S. Tell me such an institution which has free boarding and lodging facilities, and also gives some stipend to poor Muslims.

Answer: I wish you success in your life. Contact Director, Hamdard Study Circle, Talimabad, Sangam Vihar, P.O. Tughlaqabad, New Delhi-110062.

Question: I have done Fazil and have got the opportunity to study for two or three years more. Which course should I do for developing a better personality and a better career? I want to study Arabic literature with English. Which institute from among Nadwa, Jamia Nizamuddin and Jamia Millia do you think is better?

Answer: If the *madrasa* from where you did Fazil is recognised by A.M.U. Aligarh, Jamia Millia Islamia, New Delhi or by some of other universities, you can enter any one of these universities as a regular student. If not, you can pursue your career privately. There is one more institution: Please write to: Darul Umoor, Tipu Sultan Advanced Study and Research Centre, the Presidency street no-82, St. Mark Road, Bengaluru, Karnataka.

Question: I have come to know through some sources that there are some institutions which render some financial help to poor Muslim children for education. Tell me about them.

Answer: There are some institutions in various cities that offer financial help to Muslim children for their study. Contact one such institution in your city/town.

Question: Madrasa Alia, Delhi, run under Waqf Board offers eight years Maulvi course. Can a graduate of Madrasa Alia get admission to any regular or correspondence course in Jamia Millia Islamia?

Answer: You can get admission after completing Aalmiat provided that Madrasa Alia is recognised by Jamia Millia Islamia.

Question: There is a book, namely 'National Movement' in India', prescribed in Choudhari Charan Singh University, Meerut. It is for B. A. Political Science (3rd Year). It mentions on page 79 that "Ashfaqulla Khan was the first and last young man of India who sacrificed his life for the freedom of India". Can people be able to distort history?

Answer: Your concerns are laudable. It is a fact that Ashfaqulla Khan was not the first and last young Indian to lay down his life for the freedom of this country. Many Muslims took part in the freedom struggle and laid down their lives in the battles of Plassey in 1757, Sri Ranga Pattnam in 1799 and later, in 1857. But the tragedy in India is that people are engaged in distorting facts. But we should not be hopeless. Truth prevails in the long run. At the same time, it is also a painful fact that the Muslims had been sustaining irrepairably great loss.

Question: There are many colleges in our district. They have most of the subjects, except Urdu. I want Urdu to be introduced there because 42 villages of our district have Muslims in majority. What is the solution?

Answer: Contact the college administration and appeal them sincerely to introduce Urdu.

Question: When were Aligarh Muslim University and Darul Uloom Deoband established?

Answer: Aligarh Muslim University was founded in 1875, in Aligarh. Initially, it was Madrasatul Uloom. In 1877, it came to be known as Muhammadan Anglo Oriental College. In 1920, it emerged as Aligarh Muslim University. Darul Uloom Deoband was established on May 30, 1866 in Chhatte Wali Masjid by a teacher and a student. Its first student, Maulana Mahmud Hassan, was one of the prominent freedom fighters of India. He suffered imprisonment in Malta for many years due to his active participation in the freedom struggle. Darul Uloom Deoband is also known as the Al Azhar of India. Al Azhar, an Islamic University (Egypt), is of great renown.

6
Miscellaneous Questions

Question: What was the role of Sir Syed Ahmad Khan in the reformation of the Muslim society? Which educational institution did he establish?

Answer: Sir Syed Ahmad Khan introduced the Muslim society to the modern thoughts. He laid a great emphasis on the fact that the Qur'an is the word of Allah and the universe is His creation. That is why there can be no contradiction between the two. So, one's attempts to separate the religion from the world are not plausible to reason. He also played a great role in simplifying the standard of our social and cultural values and the language. In 1875, he established Madrasatul Uloom, the first institution of modern education which became Muhammadan Anglo Oriental College in 1877. It emerged as Aligarh Muslim University in 1920.

Question: Isn't it an act of great reward to sacrifice the needs and demands of one's family and society in order to propagate the message of Allah with the people engaged in Tablighi Jamaat are doing? Needless to say, they are away from their families for several months.

Answer: Propagation and the dissemination of Allah's message is a prophetic tradition. It earns one great reward. But the lives of Prophet Muhammad (Pbuh) and his companions are the best examples for us to emulate. They struck a fine balance between their responsibilities towards their families and towards Allah. Thus, they invited people towards Allah and served His slaves.

Question: Why, we don't slaughter the fish like animals to eat it?

Answer: Islam permits us to eat a dead fish because it remains healthy. It is scientifically proved that the blood of fish does not congeal in thick clots after its death. While on the other hand, the blood of other animals congeals in thick clots once they die.

Question: Some vegetable and fruit-sellers give the customers a short measure. They also play deception on the customers by selling spoiled vegetables and fruits to them. Moreover, they are also disrespectful to the customers. Give them some lovely and effective message so that they can abandon their bad habits.

Answer: The Qur'an strictly prohibits us from giving people a short measure. It is duly emphasised in the Qur'an that good conduct earns one good pleasure of Allah, who teaches us to be gentle and courteous with everyone. Those who give people a short measure and conduct badly with people, disobey both the Qur'an and all Islamic teachings. They are required to mend themselves and stay wisely mindful of their duties towards Allah and His slaves.

Question: If we make a list of the terrorists of the world, 98 per cent of them belong the Muslim families. Why is it so? Does Qur'an, your religious book, have some types of shortcomings as a book of guidance? Explain.

Answer: It is not proper to think about the Qur'an like this. These days people have deliberately created such type of atmosphere wherein every Tom, Dick and Harry is audacious enough to level false charges against Islam and the Muslims. It is a part of a propaganda campaign carried with spiteful and malicious intention against Islam. Needless to say, there are several groups of those people who are belligerently bent upon reducing the order to chaos. Their perpetrations of ruthless cruelties take toll on innocents people's death. They have open association with particular religions, but they should not be identified with their religions. And their religions are not maligned at all. One may name certain such groups: Irish Republican Army (IRA) in Northern Ireland, U.K. LTTE in Sri Lanka, Ulfa in Assam, Maoists in Nepal, Ranveer Sena and PWG in Bihar, and so on. As regards your question on the teachings of the Qur'an, it will be better if you try to see the truth it contains. The Qur'an is against any gross act of injustice, improper lifestyle and perpetration of violence. It says that killing of one innocent person amounts to the killing of the entire humanity. It is also against use of any compulsion in respect of religious matters and teachings. It teaches the believers to proclaim, "To you is your religion and to me is mine." The irony is that we are living in an age where some people are busy tearing the well-woven fabric of the society for political gains. They use religion for their petty gains. Even Hindu religion is not spared. People exploit it for their selfish motives and momentary gains. The fact is that the political system is unable to fulfill the genuine needs and wishes of the masses. If someone raises his voice against it, the cruel system subjects him to brutal tortures, aggravating the problems baying for people's blood.

Question: Is it true that most of the Indonesian know Sanskrit and Hindu culture is preserved there? Why is Urdu accorded a step-motherly treatment in India? Why are mosques and *madrasas* branded as the centres of ISI? Doesn't it seem that Islam courts danger here?

Answer: Indonesian is the official language of Indonesia. As its name reflects, it has major influence of Sanskrit. But the citizens of Indonesia do not know Sanskrit. If one believes that they know, it will amount to believing that every speaker of Urdu language knows Turkish, Persian and Arabic. Many Urdu words have been derived from these languages. In response to the question related to the step-motherly treatment, accorded to Urdu, we can say that there is a marked change in the people's attitude towards Urdu. It depends now on the speakers of Urdu to safeguard it and help it prosper more and more on the soil of India. As regards the defamation of mosques and *madrasas* to be the centres of ISI, it is a part of dirty political gimmicks. History bears witness to the fact that such things pose no threat to Islam.

Question: Does United Nations work against the Muslims? Is it obligatory for one to take a bath after one hits a pig with a stick or pelts a stone at it? Is it true that the marriage bond of a Muslim couple gets invalidated after the birth of their 20th child? Is Israel against Palestine or against Islam? Have the Muslims got the right to live in India or not? If they have the right to live here, why they are ill-treated and their integrity is suspected?

Answer: United Nations has the representatives from all Muslim countries. So, our belief that it works against the Muslim amounts to blaming ourselves. If it were true, it would not have intervened in Bosnia and Kosovo. It would not have arrested and prosecuted Slobodan Milosević in the International Tribunal. At the same time, it is significant to note that one need not agree with all the decisions of United Nations. Bath is not mandatory after hitting a pig with a stick or stone. Nikah of a couple is not invalidated after the birth of the 20th child. It seems absurd. No couple may have 20 children in India. Israel is a threat to entire humanity. Its foundation stone lies on usurpation. It is absurd to raise the questions related to the Muslims' rights to live in India. Those who look at the Muslims suspiciously and are against the Muslims, are held culprit by the Indian Constitution, civilisation and culture.

Question: There is no difference between the activities of Hindus and Muslims these days. People of both religions have wrong practices. Why should then the Muslims be termed Muslims?

Answer: I agree with you. A true Muslim always performs his obligatory duties that he owes to Allah and to his fellow human beings. Our wrong practices and evil deeds not only earn us bad reputation but also distort the true image and nature of Islam the world over.

Question: According to an Urdu-English Dictionary, the word 'Jihad' means to 'try and strive'. A Hindi-English Dictionary defines it as 'religious war'. Which one do you think is correct?

Answer: Literally, the word 'Jihad' means 'to try and strive'.

Question: Sikhs carry daggers with them and Hindu carry trishul and other weapons. Should the Muslims carry a sword with them?

Answer: If the people belonging to a particular religious sect have religious sanction to carry weapon, it is not in conformity with our religion to copy them. The Sikhs also grow hair, sport beards, possess bracelets, comb and so on. Why don't you try to copy these things? Sadly, you failed to understand the true meaning of Islam. It stands for peace, security and complete surrender and submission to the will of Allah. Bear it in mind that Islam conquered the hearts of people around the world by virtue of its courteous treatment, exemplary and ideal lifestyle of Prophet Muhammad (Pbuh) and his true followers. No sword was required to disseminate and propagate its appealing and persuasive messages.

Question: Whatever the reason, we do not know Urdu. But we have a good command on Hindi and English. During our discussions with the so-called and self-professed leaders of Islam, they tell us that we are not true Muslims because we do not know Urdu. We think Urdu is just a language. It has nothing to do with Islam and its messages. It is not the language of Islam. What is your opinion?

Answer: I agree with you. A language has no religion. In other words, religion does not consist in a language. Every religion needs a language, as a medium for its propagation and dissemination. It is absurd to say that one cannot be a good Muslim unless one knows a particular language. It is true that here, the books on every aspect of Islamic knowledge are largely available in Urdu. And they are as authentic as any book in Persian and Arabic. But it is significant to mention that most of the books on Islamic literature in India were published by a Hindu, Munshi Nawal Kishore, Lucknow. We should also have it in mind that Urdu was also used as a medium of the propagation of many other religions. The irony is that in India many times, languages are wrongly identified with religions and it is believed that Urdu is the language of the Muslims and Hindi, the language of the Hindus. We should demolish the typical narrow-mindedness otherwise we will be deprived of 'Gulzar-e-Naseem' by Pandit Daya Shankar Nasim, 'Ramayan ka Ek Scene' by Brij Narayan Chakbast, high class poetry by Raghupati Sahai Firaq, urdu novels by Krishna Chandar and Rajendra Singh Bedi. Similarly, Hindi will be deprived of the classical Muslim poets like Malik Muhammad Jaisi, Raheem, Ras Khan and decent fiction by Abdul Bismillah, Mahrunnisa Parvez and Asghar Wajahat and so on.

Question: It is said that the terrorists have no religion. If it is so, why are the Muslims branded as terrorists? You say that no good and true Muslim can be a terrorist. Wasn't Osama bin Laden, the most terrible terrorist of the world, a good Muslim? He had killed millions of people in the name of Islam.

Answer: I have been answering such types of questions for quite some time now. Perhaps my answers are not clear enough to make some folks understand my viewpoints. It may be that some of them are not ready to agree with me. I will only be repeating myself today. Islam which means peace and security has nothing to do with terrorism. It ensures people their civil rights, equality and peace. Isn't it ironical that the people associated with ULFA or Bodoland in Assam are not branded as the Hindu terrorists. Similarly, the people associated with IRA in Ireland are not identified as Catholic Christian terrorists. People are politically motivated, when they identify terrorism or terrorists with Islam. Those people who level the charges of terrorism against the Muslims are in the know of the fact that it is completely rubbish to identify a religion or a sect with the terrorism and terrorists. I am still of the opinion that a true Muslim can't be a terrorist. Islam says in clear terms that killing of one innocent person amounts to the killing of the entire humanity and the act of saving one innocent person amounts to saving the entire humanity.

Question: Signature in Urdu is acceptable in the banks of Uttar Pradesh. Is it also acceptable in other states? Blocks and police stations have Urdu translators. Why aren't the translators appointed in the banks? In Muslim majority, areas people sign in Urdu. When the photo of an account holder who signs in Urdu becomes old, the members of bank staff do not authenticate the signature. They do authenticate, if the account holders sign in English. Isn't it an act of gross injustice to Urdu?

Answer: Signature in Urdu is acceptable in all Indian banks. If a bank is doing so, it is an act of discrimination against Urdu knowing persons. We should raise our voice against it. Urdu is one of 22 recognised national languages of India.

Question: The leader of the prayer in our village mosque has got his name tattooed on his hand. Is it permissible for a Muslim to have one's name tattooed on one's hand. Is it permissible for one to pray under his leadership?

Answer: It is not proper for a Muslim to have his name or something else tattooed on the body. But there is no harm in performing one's pray led by an Imam who got it tattooed in his childhood. But then, he should bring himself to a sincere repentance.

Question: What is the population of the Muslims in Indonesia and India?

Answer: According to the official data (1990), the population of Muslims in Indonesia was 18 million. According to the 1991 census of India, the population of the Muslims in India was 120 million.

Question: Most of us say that we should eat from 'halal'—lawful earning. Here, lawful earning stands for money earned through hard labour and in an honest way. Isn't it ironical that the Muslims believe their act of slaughtering animals to be 'halal'. They kill the animals mercilessly. Allah does not like violence against innocent humans or animals. Then why is it so?

Answer: The literal meaning of 'halal' understood by you is correct. As far as your criticism of slaughtering the animals is concerned, I can only say that even medical science has declared this way of slaughtering animals to be better. It is so because the blood of the animal which may be harmful for those who eat their meat flows out of its body.

Question: Amir Khusrow was a great saint. He had an association with *durbar* as well, although he never liked to be associated with the king and his *durbar*. Hazrat Nizamuddin Auliya, the spiritual guide of Amir Khusrow, was also against the association with kings and their *durbar*. Then why was Amir Khusrow associated with *durbar*?

Answer: Amir Khusrow was associated with the durbar of only one King, rather with the *durbars* of many kings. But he was emotionally and truly associated with Hazrat Nizamuddin Auliya. Almost all Sufi saints used to keep themselves away from kings and their *durbars*. Some Sufis thought it was improper for them to have association with the kings. Hazrat Amir

Khusrow had the permission of Hazrat Nizamuddin Auliya, for it. It is also worth mentioning here that he remained associated with *durbar* but he never compromised his Sufi ideologies, literary points of view and love for music. Though he had association with the people in politics those days, he was as clean as a lotus in muddy water.

Question: Is it right for the Muslim students and officers to pray during their classes and duty hours? What should we prefer, religion or duty?

Answer: By chance, no prayer time clashes with the study or duty hours. Take for example, Zuhr prayer. It is performed during the lunch break. As regards choice between religion and work, according to Islamic teachings true religion consists in practical deeds.

Question: Whenever a problem about Urdu comes to the surface, it is said that no religious literature of the Muslims will exist without the existence of Urdu. It will be a great loss. On the other hand, it is also said that Urdu is not the language of the Muslims alone. Aren't these things self-contradictory?

Answer: The question you have raised is very important. We need to contemplate. It is true that the religious literature produces in Urdu is not equal to Islamic literature in Arabic and Persian languages. But Urdu language too has very important and significant books on Islam. No doubt, if the Urdu language becomes extinct, it will be a great loss. It won't be a loss for the Muslims alone, it will also be an irrepairable loss to the composite culture of the Indian sub-continent. However, it is important to note that Urdu has made a great contribution to the propagation of all religious traditions in India. One may, for example, quote the Geeta, the Ved, the Ramayana, and the Mahabharata and other Hindu religious books, which have several versions of translations in Urdu. The translation of the Bible is also available in Urdu. Similarly, one can easily trace several Urdu words in the Guru Granth Sahib. Besides, verses of many Sikh Gurus are basically in Urdu. Evidently enough, attaching Urdu with a particular religion is not proper. Interestingly, it was Munshi Nawal Kishore, a publisher of Lucknow, who published the most important books on Islam and the Muslim civilisation.

Question: Who wrote Vande Matram? When and why?

Answer: Shri Bankim Chandra Chatterjee wrote Vande Matram. It occurs in his famous novel 'Anand Math'. This novel presents the ways one's motherland is worshipped in. It is in conformity with Hinduism. It is significant to mention here that Islam teaches one to worship Allah alone.

Since such worshipful attitude towards the motherland is contrary to the spirit of the basic articles of Islamic beliefs, the Muslims have reservations. They can't sing it while accepting anything else other than Allah to be worthy of worship. I would like emphasise upon the fact that it never makes a Muslim fail, in staying loyal and patriotic to his country.

Question: You say that Islam doesn't teach rigidity and ruthlessness. But whenever there is a riot in a city, curfew is clamped in the Muslim areas, and they are declared very sensitive? areas as well. Tell me why only the areas with the Muslims in majority are declared sensitive. The Hindus and the followers of other religions never create great havoc as the Muslims. Why is it so?

Answer: Imposition of curfew during the riots only in the areas with the Muslims in majority is the result of the mindset of the police force and district administration. It is absurd to believe the Muslims to be ruthless because of the teachings of Islam. The places where the police officials and district administration work impartially, never witness any untoward happenings. To learn about the mindset of the police officials and their line of action, one should read Vibhuti Narayan Rai's novel 'Shahar Mein Curfew' (Curfew in the City).

Question: When compared to a Christian calendar year, a Hijri calendar year has ten days less in a year. It seems to be unscientific. Why didn't people pay attention to remove the shortcoming?

Answer: Hijri calendar is based on the phases of the moon. So, it differs to a solar calendar. To call it unscientific is not proper. There are also some other calendars like Shak and Vikrami. They too differ from the Christian calendar. They have eight or ten days less in a year. Even in solar calendar, the year after four years has one more added day. The speed and rotation of moon is scientifically proved.

Question: I am a T.B. patient. Due to poverty I am unable to undergo the treatment. There is a doctor who advised me to eat snails. Is it permissible for a Muslim to eat snail?

Answer: There are so many centres where T.B. patients receive free treatment. But if a doctor thinks that your illness cannot be cured by any other treatment except for eating the snail for medicinal purpose, it is permissible for you until you are cured.

Question: Even a illiterate person can understand the meaning of poem 'Sare Jahan Se Achcha', written by Allama Iqbal. But even a knowledgeable person is unable to understand the meaning of the national song 'Jana Gana Mana Adhinayak' written by Rabindra Nath Tagore. Tell me its meaning.

Answer: Iqbal's national song 'Sare Jahan Se Achcha' is written in Urdu or in Gandhiji's language—'Hindustani'. It is a song about the national bravery, its renown and power of tolerance. This language is spoken and understood in large parts of our country. Rabindra Nath Tagore's 'Jana Gana Mana is our national song. This is about geographical vastness and greatness of India. Originally, it is in Bangla language which has been translated in Sanskritised Hindi. This is the reason, it is not understood by those who do not know the language, well.

Question: As you treat yourself to be from a minority group, there are other people who also treat themselves to be from the minority group. Why don't you have the same kind of feeling and sympathy for them?

Answer: We feel concerned not on the basis of minority and majority but on the basis of problems encountering people. We genuinely feel that everyone should get the equal opportunity to develop and prosper, and be able to contribute one's share towards the development of the country. We sincerely wish that no one is denied justice and civil and other rights.

Question: Prof. Wasey, the people of our country have faced communal riots several times. We feel that you do not have any hatred and anger towards the Hindus. It is laudable. Muslims think that the discriminatory attitude towards them is the root cause of their poverty. We have seen that they always discuss the topics concerning prayers and fasting. But they never discuss the importance of education. It is surprising when one sees a Muslim business man going to join a *tableeghi* team for 40 days – that too entrusting his business to someone else. It means that religion is more important than the world.

Answer: Thank you very much. It is true that I do not feel agitated, when I see riots against the Muslims. But I feel concerned and sad. I do not accuse all the Hindus. As regards the education among the Muslims, people have been trying their best to carry the campaign of Sir Syed Ahmad Khan so that the Muslim masses do not stand aloof from the mainstream education and contemporary development. If a businessman has made some proper arrangement, there is no harm if he joins *Jamaat* and spends 40 days there on the path of Allah. One has spiritual as well as material needs and one needs both types of satisfactions.

Question: The verdict given by the court in Shah Bano's case was correct. It proved to be the Muslims' sycophancy to get the verdict invalidated. Justice has no concern with religion.

Answer: No one aimed to disrespect the court by getting its verdict invalidated. In fact, the bench had interpreted some verses of the Qur'an in a way which was unacceptable to the Muslims. Thus, the interpretation gave way to the new conflict. Refusing to accept the court's interpretation of those verses of the Qur'an, the scholars of Islam stood to oppose the verdict of the court. They held it as interference with the Muslim personal laws. In view of the Muslims' sentiments, the Indian government passed an amendment in the Constitution to quash the verdict of the court. I don't agree with your point of view that justice has no concern with religion. Justice is an integral part of religion. No religion can survive without justice as its vital feature.

Question: I have come to know that no Hindu lives in Makkah and Madinah. They have no permission to go there. Why? In India, Muslims can go to any sacred place.

Answer: No non-Hindu is allowed to go inside Shri Jagannath temple in Puri and also inside Venkateshwara temple in Tirupati. Similarly, no non-Parsis are allowed entry inside Parsi worship houses.

Question: Tell the address of National Minority Commission. How does it function and what kinds of assistance does it provide?

Answer: The Address is as follows:

National Minority Commission
Lok Nayak Bhawan, Khan Market
New Delhi-110003

You may get further information, if you write a letter to its secretary.

Question: How about introducing a religion, religion of humanity, which consists of people belonging to every religion? If we have such a religion there, won't be any conflicts in the name of Mandir-Masjid, religion, culture and so on. Can you give your suggestions?

Answer: I appreciate your feelings but such efforts are bound to fail. It will end the independence of thought and action in the areas of religion and culture. It will curb people's freedom and stunt the growth of their thoughts. Moreover, the thing which has not been declared essential by the Creator of the Universe, should not be our coveted goal. It is not natural. If one common religion had been the source of peace, well-being, amity and brotherhood, then, differences and conflicts among the people of various religions would not have existed in the world.

Question: Isn't the Indian Constitution secular? If it had been secular, 'Satya Mev Jaitey' would not have the emblem of India. The word 'Satya' traces its origin in Sanatan Vedic religion. Secondly, if it had been a secular country, word from different religious books would have also been mentioned.

Answer: No religion has monopoly on truth. The grandeur of truth remains intact; no matter whether it is expressed in Hindi or any other language. I do not agree with your views regarding 'Satya Mev Jaitey'. Every religion teaches us that the truth prevails in the long run. Our national emblems are our common national heritage. We must accord respect to them.

Question: Tell the address of the Waqf Board in Delhi so that matters concerning the problems of graveyard, houses and illegal possessions can be brought to its notice.

Answer: The address is as follows:
Delhi Waqf Board
Bachchon Ka Ghar
Darya Ganj, New Delhi-110002

Question: Where there is terrorism, there is Islamic Jihad. Why shouldn't we conclude that Islamic Jihad is terrorism and terrorism is Islamic Jihad?

Answer: One's act of considering terrorism as Islamic Jihad is but a gross mistake. Islam has no place for terrorism. As regards the meaning of Jihad, the greatest form of Jihad consists in one's act of waging war against deadly sins like pride and arrogance, avarice, carnal desires, jealousy and so on. As regards fighting against people for self-defence, for establishment of peace and so on, there is a strict prohibition of fighting with children, old men and women, ailing and weak people and pious people retiring in the worship houses for worshipful devotion, as also against those who do not confront. Islam warns us against spoiling the crops and gardens. Islam hates ruthless carnage, animalism and indiscriminate killing and the act of carrying out arson attacks. It teaches us that the limit set by Allah should be transgressed under no circumstances. It also does not allow one to fight against the wounded soldiers, fugitives and captives. Moreover, those who run away and close their doors will obtain security and protection. Furthermore, The Qur'an brands the murder a greater mischief than '*kufr*'. In view of the above, one will wisely avoid identifying terrorism with Islamic Jihad. Needless to say, it will be a gross injustice to Islam and its followers.

Question: How many months does a Hijri calendar year have? Write their names and number of days.

Answer: A Hijri calendar year consists of 12 months. The months are of 29 or 30 days. The names of the months are Muharram-ul-Haram, Safar-al-Muzaffar, Rabiul Awwal, Rabiussani, Jamadiul Awwal, Jamdiussani, Rajabul Murajjab, Sha'banul Moazzam, Ramzanul Mubarak, Shawwalul Mukarram, Zul Qadah and Zil Hijj.

Question: Can an M.L.A. of Uttar Pradesh take oath in Urdu? If not, why? Why are oaths taken by putting one's hand on religious books?

Answer: Oaths can not be taken in Urdu, in U.P. because its official language is Hindi. The tradition of putting one's hand is due to the assumption that one who takes oath with his hands on the religious book will be true to his words.

Question: Due to the narrow mindedness, many Muslim brothers do not go to temples. And Hindus can't go to Muslim worship houses. Our national leaders teach that religions do not teach us to nurse ill-will against one another. Even Bapu said 'Ishwar Allah tero naam, Sab ko Sanmati De Bhagwan'. What is your opinion about it?

Answer: The act of not going to others' religious places is not narrow mindedness. It is an issue related to faith. One can co-exist with peace, amity and brotherhood even after one's true attachment to one's religious beliefs and faiths. Gandhi ji recited 'Ishwar Allah Tero Naam' as a prayer to God. He wanted to impart a sense of togetherness. It was a message to us that whatever name we use for invoking God, we should remain in peace and harmony for the social advancement.

Question: Should religious scholars take part in politics?

Answer: In my opinion, taking part in politics as a common citizen has no harm. But we should have in mind that religious values and beliefs should not be exploited for the political ends. If one exploits religion for political ends, it provokes communalism.

Question: I have heard that it is also a duty of Maulvis and religious leaders to educate the people. In Pakistan, their names are identified with the terrorist organisations. What is your opinion?

Answer: Certainly, it is the duty of religious scholars to give religious education because it creates a good atmosphere with the help of making people good and pious. As regards Pakistan, it should be kept in mind that the persons having association with the terrorists, are not the representatives of religion. They are known as political leaders, not as scholars of Islam.

Question: What is the definition of 'terrorism'? There should be a national discourse on it. Any group or person who strictly follows Islam is branded as terrorist or extremist by these fascists.

Answer: Terrorism is a subject of discussion at national as well as international levels. Islamic way of life and the propagation of Islamic beliefs have nothing to do with the terrorism. The rigidity and orthodoxy pave the way for terrorism. We all should wisely avoid it for the health of our society.

Question: How many Muslim countries are there in the world? Which country is the richest among them?

Answer: There are 56 Islamic countries in the world. Darussalam Brunei situated in South-East Asia is considered to be the richest among them.

Question: How many people of the minority community might have received help from National Minority Development Finance Commission? Its Chairman was Qari Muhammad Mian.

Answer: The commission was established on 30th January, 1996. Till March 2000, it had distributed 224.34 crore rupees among 66091 persons from 21 states through its SCA programme. To know more about its objectives and activities, you may contact National Minority Development Finance Commission, I A, Taimoor Nagar, Opposite D 996, New Friends Colony, New Delhi-110065.

Question: What was the official language of the Mughals? Urdu was born out of interaction between Hindu and Muslim culture. Why is Urdu receiving step-motherly treatment? The government says that the number of Urdu speaking persons is very low, whereas most of the religious body of knowledge is in Urdu. What do you think?

Answer: The official language of the Mughals was Persian. No doubt, Urdu played a vital role in the interaction and cultural exchanges. But it has continuously been receiving step-motherly treatment since independence. The intention and policies of government are not good. But we, the speakers of Urdu, are equally responsible for its deterioration. We have been very hesitant in admitting our children and wards in the schools where, the medium of instruction and examination is Urdu. But the situation is changing for good and Urdu is regaining its previous status.

Question: Is the massacre of the Muslims in Gujarat going to pave way to another partition?

Answer: It is an undeniable truth that most of the intellectuals, journalists, people, fighting for human rights and social workers of the country and even the judiciary took the massacre to have brought ill-reputation to the country and put it to disgrace in the eyes of the world. It is a slur on our system. As far as the division of the country is concerned, no one can be successful in his heinous plan. Allama Iqbal rightly said, 'Kuch Baat hai ki hasti mit ti nahi hasti hamari/Sadiyon raha hai dushman daur-e-zaman hamara.

Question: After Gujarat riots, the Muslims were paid Rs. 200 as compensation in place of 2 lakhs. Isn't it a gross act of injustice and partiality? People like you are but mere spectators?

Answer: The whole world knows the act of gross injustice and partiality meted out to the victims of Gujarat riots. The human rights commission, a constitutional body, is a witness to it. During riots I went to Vadrodra, Godhra, Lunawara, Ahmadabad, etc. and extended the possible help with the help of different organisations. We do not believe in publicity.

Question: When did the Hijri year start? In which year was Prophet Muhammad (Pbuh) born?

Answer: Hijri year started the day Prophet Muhammad (Pbuh) migrated to Madinah from Makkah. It was initiated by Hazrat Umar Farooq, one of the caliphs. Prophet Muhammad (Pbuh) was born long before the beginning of the Hijri year. According to the Christian year, it was April 571.

Question: Why did the Muslim leaders demanding punishment to be meted out to the people involved in Gujarat riots keep mum on the killings of innocent people in Chittisinghpura and Amarnath pilgrims in Kashmir?

Answer: The killing of innocent people, be it in Chittisinghpura, Amarnath or in Gujarat, is a gross act of brutality. It must be condemned. No one involved in such heinous crimes should be spared. Muslim leaders have always condemned such types of crimes. The irony is that their statements and views are published only in Urdu newspapers. God knows why they do not get space in Hindi and English newspapers. This is the reason that their views, feelings and thoughts do not reach the non-Urdu speaking people. It creates a wide gulf, leading to an atmosphere, where people regard one another with suspicion. The central government is requested to gather the views of the Muslim leaders and intellectuals on every communal riot that took place during last fifteen years, and publish a white paper so that the responses and viewpoints of the Muslim leaders and intellectuals may be known to the public.

Question: A mosque is a religious place. Many times, people sleep thereafter their work or duty.

Answer: A mosque is house of Allah. In olden times, it used to be the centre of the Muslim culture. There is no harm, if a traveller or a votary of prayer stays there for a while to rest. But it is not proper for one to make it one's permanent resting place and treat it to be one's private place.

Question: Is there any country in the world where there is not even a single follower of Islam?

Answer: I do not know about a country where there is no Muslim.

Question: I have some very close Muslim friends. After the organised riot by Gujarat Government, there is a marked change in their behaviours and thoughts. They do not trust me now. Why am I being penalised for being a Hindu? I am completely a secular person and consider Islam as the best religion.

Answer: I feel embarrassed. If the thinking of your friends is such, as you have said, they should not forget that their behaviour is against the teachings and spirit of Islam. They should not forget that people belonging to the Hindu community raised their voice against the massacre. Many of them staged demonstrations to express their sorrow and anger. Under the Chairmanship of justice Verma, National Human Rights Commission, prosecuted the Gujarat government. It is significant to mention that Hindu community also has the majority of those people who are, like any good Muslim, Christian and so on—secular in true sense of the word. They are staunch supporters of unity, peace, brotherhood, amity and harmony among the people of different communities. Those who were involved in the heinous genocide of the Muslims, were not Hindus by belief. They were nothing but a blot on the image of India. They should not be identified with general Hindus of Gujarat.

Question: Can a Muslim become the Prime Minister in India? Is it possible to have a Muslim regiment in Indian army? Please answer in the light of Indian Constitution. From where can I get a copy of our Constitution?

Answer: A copy of Indian Constitution can be purchased from a book shop in the market. As regards a Muslim's becoming the Prime Minister, it is not impossible. Having a regiment of particular religion is out of question in a secular country like ours. Even in the past, there was no such regiment. We have a Sikh regiment but the cause behind it is historical not religious.

Question: What are the meanings of words 'Kafir' and Jihad'? Some Hindus are still confused. These words are often misunderstood.

Answer: The meaning of the word 'Kafir' has already been given. The word 'Jihad' literally means 'exertion and striving of a very high order'. For a , it denotes one's endeavour against one's baser self in order to curb and tune it with worshipful virtuousness for the pleasure of Allah. Our Hindu brothers may understand it as exertion of one's power against acts of gross injustice, evil and exploitative practices. A person having strong faith in the Geeta, cannot oppose Jihad. In the battle of *Kurukshetra,* the arguments given by Lord Krishna to Pandavas for fighting against Kauravas initially aimed at fighting against injustice might and men. In fact, Jihad consists in the act of fighting against evil, injustice, tyranny, exploitation and a host of other vices.

Question: Who built Jama Masjid and the Lal Qila (Delhi)? Who was its first Imam?

Answer: The world famous mosque, Jama Masjid of Delhi, is also called Shahjahani Mosque. Shahjahan, a Mughal King, built it. Syed Abdul Ghafoor Bukhari was its first Imam. The present Imam Syed Ahmad Bukhari is from among the thirteenth generation of Syed Ghafoor. The Lal Qila was also built by Shahjahan.

Question: People started practising witchcraft after it was introduced to them by evil spirits. Who practised it for the first time?

Answer: According to Islamic traditions, it were Haroot and Maroot who practised it for the first time on the earth.

Question: What are the names by which Baba Adam and mother Hawwa are known by the Hindus?

Answer: There can be no authentic answer. According to Hindu traditions, the human race was perpetuated by Manu and Shat Roopa.

Question: Some of my friends say about Indian Muslims that they eat from their earnings in India but feel concerned about Makkah and Madinah. But when such Indian Muslims start criticising India and praising Pakistan, I also doubt their intention. What is your opinion about such Muslims?

Answer: Today, the world has been reduced to a global village. The thought about Indian Muslims that they eat in India and feel concerned about Makkah and Madinah is in no way positive and acceptable. The followers of no religion can detach themselves from their holy places. Aren't the places like Amarnath, Badrinath, Haridwar, Kashi, Prayag, Tirupati, etc. holy places for the devotees living in America, Europe and other countries of the world. Makkah and Madinah are as important for Muslims as are Bathlehem and Vatican city for the Christians. As far as Pakistan is concerned, no Indian Muslim praises it on the basis of religion and emotions. Some people may feel a bond with their relatives living in Pakistan. Those who eulogise Pakistan and condemn India are to be condemned in true sense of the word.

Question: There is a mosque near Qutub Minar. Its name is 'Quwwatul Islam'. It means power of Islam. This mosque was constructed with the ruins of temples. It does not stand for the power of Islam but for the power of its followers. Doesn't it prove that Islam was not propagated by virtue of love but by the power of the sword?

Answer: Islam is against doing any harm to the worship houses of any religion. No Muslim is allowed to demolish others' worship houses and convert them into his worship houses. It must be kept in mind that Islam was propagated by virtue of its practical approaches towards equality, kindness and love. True Islam consists not in the soldiers but in Sufis and their lives. It is not easy to reach the truth of medieval period. It is better for us to ward off our past from our mind to live and make sincere efforts towards the development of the present and future India.

Question: Assalam Alaikum is considered as greeting to the group of people. Salam refers to greeting a single person. 'Wa Alaikum Assalam' is the response to 'Assalam Alaikum'. Is it right to say Salam in response to Salam?

Answer: 'Assalam Alaikum' means "May God bless and protect you all'. It means that it is for a single person as well as for the whole group of people. We should say 'Wa Alaikum Assalam' in response to 'Salam' as well. It also means "May God bless and protect you all'. We should always utter complete wishing words in response to 'Salam'.

Question: How and why are some persons, who have no knowledge of Islam, able to tarnish the image of Islam by dint of dominating the Muslim leaders?

Answer: It is not the tragedy Islam alone. Other religions also face this problem. There are some people who want to serve their political ends for making money. They provoke general masses in the name of religion. So, it is necessary that the Muslims and people of other religions should unite to fight these people and protect their religions against exploitation. At the same time, they should also try their best to highlight and propagate the true spirit of religion which consists in dedicated devotion to God, philanthropy and service to humanity.

Question: I was a non-Muslim. I have converted to Islam. I pray five daily prayers and recite the Qur'an as well. My husband gets frightened during his sleep. He wants to work but he gets distracted, sometimes he loses his jobs. I have been reciting the verses of the Qur'an and blowing on him, but to no effect.

Answer: Consult a good psychiatrist. Everything will be alright.

Question: Please do not write the names of Allah and the Prophet in newspapers. People generally throw them here and there. It causes disrespect.

Answer: We do try our best to safeguard the names of Allah and His Prophet against being disrespected. But it is not wrong to write the names of Allah and His Prophet for good purposes. God knows the innermost intentions of His slaves.

Question: Though Islam ruled over the whole world, other religions are still practised in different parts of the world. Is it due to the weakness of its preachers or the religion itself?

Answer: The survival of other religions under the Islamic rule should not be treated as the weakness of Islam or its preachers. It is the fundamental teachings of Islam that there is no compulsion in the matter of religion. So, no one allowed to use force or compulsion for the propagation, nor one allowed to hurl foul words at others' gods and religions. God sent down His prophets to every community for the guidance of the people. This is the spirit of a religion so that the people of other religions also flourish under the Islamic rule. Thus, it should not be treated as weakness.

Question: Is there anything like witchcraft or evil spirit? If yes, what is its treatment in the light of the Qur'an and the prophetic traditions? Is it right to use amulets? Can one take amulets from those people who do not charge money for it?

Answer: Yes, witchcraft and evil spirits do exist. They are harmful for the health of human beings. According to the prophetic tradition, one should recite *Surah Falaq and Surah Naas* to save oneself from the witchcraft and the evil spirits. There are some other prayers too which serve as the antidote to the effect of the witchcraft. There is no harm in consulting an elderly and knowledgeable person. But it is not permissible to make it one's profession.

Question: What does Islam say about the persons who do not respond to the greeting (salam)? What is the role of a messenger through whom one sends one's greeting to others?

Answer: One's act of not responding back someone's greeting is against Islamic teachings and culture. It is a good act to convey other's salam. If one forgets to convey it, one should try to convey it as soon as it is possible. The act of not conveying one's greeting intentionally is against the ethics.

Question: When someone accepts Islam, he keeps a new name. And the name generally happens to be some Arabic name. The Arabic names of the Muslims were the names of their pre-Islamic ancestors who were the worshippers of many idols and gods. After the advent of Islam, they did not change their names. But the Indian Muslims change their Indian names after embracing Islam. Is is true?

Answer: It is correct to have names from any language. But the meaning of the name should be good. It should not be against basic Islamic beliefs. The change of name is not necessary, if old name is not against the fundamental Islamic beliefs.

Question: Mr. Vibhuti Narain Rai, Inspector General of Police (Uttar Pradesh), has written in his book 'Communal Riots and Indian Police' that the number of Muslims in police department is very less. This is the reason that the police do acts of gross injustice to them. What is your opinion?

Answer: Mr. Vibhuti Narain Rai is one of the senior police officers. Whatever he has written is based on his personal experiences. He has introduced us to the basic causes of the communal riots and the government machinery. Now, it depends on us to take the remedial measures in this regard.

Glossary

Halala: It refers to the process which a husband who wants to remarry his divorcee has to adopt. If a husband pronounces talaq three times, his wife stays divorced. He is not allowed to remarry her immediately after divorce. The divorced woman has to marry another man. Now, if she is divorced by him or she is widowed, her previous husband can remarry her.

Halal: All those lawful things and acts that have Islamic sanctions are known as Halal (permissible).

Haram: All those unlawful things and acts which have no sanction in Islamic laws are Haram (forbidden).

Wahy: Literally it means to hint but in Islamic terminology, it implies the messages sent by Allah to His messengers and prophets.

Al Hamd: The first Surah which the Qur'an begins with. Its theme is *Al Fatah.* Since this Surah starts with the word 'Al Hamd', it is commonly known as Surah *Al Fatiha.*

Surah Ikhlas: It is Surah number 112. Its theme is '*ikhlas*', which means purity (of Faith). It describes the Oneness of Allah. The belief in His oneness is the most important part of the pure faith.

Shariat: Islamic laws or Islamic system of life.

Tareeqat: Literally it means 'path' or 'way'. In Islamic terminology, it stands for *Tasawwuf* (Islamic mysticism).

Rak'at: It stands for a cycle of prayer which includes the act of standing for prayer, bowing down, prostrating with ones nose and forehead resting on the earth. A prayer can consist of 2, 3 or 4 *rak'ats.*

Hadith: Saying and doing of Hazrat Muhammad (Pbuh), as also his silent approbation of the acts and statements to his companions.

Sunnat: The traditions and acts of Prophet Muhammad (Pbuh).

Fiqh: Literally it means 'to understand'. In Islamic terminology, it refers to the jurisprudence of the Muslim laws, civil as well as criminal. It also implies the act of deduction of solutions to the civil and religious issues in the light of the Qur'an and Hadith. It other words, it is the act of making Islamic laws.

Hanafi, Shafai, Maliki, Humbali: They refer to four different personalities who contributed their share towards the evolution and making of Islamic laws. The Muslims follow them. By extension, they refer to four different schools of thought. The founder of Hanafi school of thought was Imam Abu Haneefa. Imam Muhammad bin Idrees Shafai founded Shafai school of thought. Maliki school of thought was founded by Imam Malik bin Anas and Ahmad Bin Hambal was the founder of Hambali school of thought. There are also other schools of thought like Ahl-e-Hadith, Fiqh- e-Jafri and so on.

Zinakari: It means adultery. Islam has prescribed strict punishments for this hatefully condemnable act.

Shirk: It means polytheism. In Islamic terminology, it refers to the act of ascribing plurality to Allah and also considering someone else other than Allah to be worthy of worship.

Mushrik: It refers to a polytheist, one who associates partners with Allah.

Dul Dul: It was the name of the horse of Hazrat Ali, the son-in-law of Prophet Muhammad (Pbuh). He was the fourth caliph of Islam.

Burraq: The creature which Prophet Muhammad (Pbuh) used for the celestial ascension (Meraj).

Namaz: The word '*Namaz*' refers to '*Salah*' in Arabic. It means prayer. It is one of the five important pillars of Islam. Five daily prayers are obligatory on Muslims. They are as follows: 1. *Fajr* (from dawn until the sunrise). 2. *Zuhr* (from early afternoon before the time of *Asr* prayer) 3. *Asr* (from late afternoon until before *Maghrib* prayer). 4. *Maghrib* (just after the sunset. Its time expires after 1 hour and 30 minutes from the sunset) 5. *Isha* (from the first part of the night until the midnight). There are certain more prayers which are not obligatory. It is significant to mention that a Muslim is not allowed to prostrate before Allah at the time of the sunrise and the sunset.

Darul Har'b: It refers to such a political and geographical area where cruelties are perpetrated on Muslims and they are not allowed to practice their religious rituals. Since they are denied religious rights, they are forced to wage war for their rights.

Durood: It refers to the act of invoking Allah's blessings to Prophet Muhammad (Pbuh). According to the Qur'an, Allah and His angels honour and bless Prophet Muhammad (Pbuh) by sending blessings on him. The believers are commanded to send blessings and salute him with all due respect. This command of Allah occurs in Surah: *Al- Ahzab*, Verse: 56. The expression *Sal lallaho Alaihe Wassallam* stands for blessing and salute to Prophet Muhammad (Pbuh).

Iddat: It is probation incumbent on a woman in case her husband dies or her husband divorces her. A woman, whose husband dies, has to stay inside her house for four months and ten days. In case of divorce, iddat is for three months. It has been enjoined upon these women by Allah. In case a woman is on a family way, she is not allowed to marry until the delivery of the child.

Kaffarah: The word '*kaffarah*' has been derived from '*takfeer*'. It literally means to wipe out. In the terminology of Islamic Sharia, it refers to expiation or atonement.

Istinja: It implies the act of obtaining purity or cleanliness after defication or unination.

Arkaan: The word '*arkaan*' is the plural form of '*rukn*'. It means some vital constituents or important conditions.

Ummat: Community, followers of a religion.

Aqeeqah: When a baby is born to Muslim parents, they express their thankfulness to Allah by slaughtering a sacrificial animal. It is generally performed on the 7th day or the child's birth. This ceremony is known as *Aqeeqah*.

Fazil: Literally it means a great scholar of Islam. This word also refers to the highest Madrasa degree.

Aalim: Literally it means a person of great knowledge. It also refers to a Madrasa degree conferred before 'Fazil'.

Hadiyah: Gift.

Maslak: Path or religious sect.

Kafir: It stands for one who denies the Truth (Allah).

Talaaq: It is a prescribed way for the dissolution of marriage. Only husbands reserve this right. According to the meaning of a Hadith, it is the most detestable permissible act in the sight of Allah.

Khulaa: It stands for the right of a wife to take release from the marriage by getting the contract terminated.

Munafiq: Literally it means malicious and hypocrite. In Islamic terminology, it stands for those hypocrites who pretended to be Muslim but plotted against Islam.

Sadaqah: The charity dispensed in the path of Allah.

Fitrah: It refers to the charity dispensed before the performance of Eid prayer. The objective of *Fitrah* is to help poor people celebrate Eid.

Ajr: Reward, a good return.

Qada: Missing the prescribed time of any five daily prayer and fast. A votary of prayer performs it and observes the fast on some later time or day.

Deobandi: The followers of *Darul Uloom* Deoband.

Barelvi: Those who follow Aala Hazrat Ahmad Raza Khan Barelvi. He was a great scholar of Islam. Barelvis prefer to be called as *Ahl-e-Sunnat wal Jamaat*.

Muslim: It refers to one who believes in Islam.

Ghair Muslim: It stands for those who believe in religions other than Islam.

Shia: An Islamic sect which gives priority to Hazrat Ali in the matter of *Imamat*. Shias believe in 12 *Imams*. This sect has different subsects like Ismaili, Dawoodi, Zaidi, etc.

Sunni: An Islamic sect. Sunnis believe in caliphate as per the historical order. They accord due respect to *Ahl-e-Bait* and *Imams*.

Hajj: It stands for the pilgrimage to the holy house of Allah in Makkah situated in Saudi Arabia. It involves compulsory rituals like staying on the plain of Arafat, Mina and Muzdalifah, as also the performance of other compulsory and non-compulsory rituals. This journey is undertaken and rituals are performed on the prescribed date in the month of Zil Hijjah, the last month of the Islamic calendar.

Muharram: It is the first month of the Islamic calendar. On the tenth of Muharram, the adversaries of Islam perpetrated cruelties on Imam Husain and his people, and subjected them to indignities. They martyred them brutally.

Taazia: It refers to a symbolic structure made to commemorate Imam Husain and his martyrdom.

Nikah: It refers to the marriage bond in which a male and a female enter as per the norms prescribed by Islam.

Assalam Alaikum: It stands for sending Allah's blessings. People exchange this Islamic greetings, when they meet or take leave. The one who greets first says *Assalam Alaikum* (May you be granted peace!). The person who is greeted responds by *Wa Alaikum Assalam.* (May you also be granted peace!)

Khatna: Chopping off the foreskin of the male reproductive organ. It is the tradition of Hazrat Ibrahim (a.s.), which is followed by Jews, Christians, as well as Muslims.

Kausar: It is the name of a fountain. It will be the only source of water on the day of judgement. According to *Surah-Al-Kausar*, it has been given to Prophet Muhammad (Pbuh). According to a Hadith, he (Pbuh) will offer water from it to the believers.

Makkah: Situated in Saudi Arabia, it is a holy place where Prophet Muhammad (Pbuh) was born. He lived there for 53 years until his migration to Madinah. This city is one of the two most sacred places for the Muslims, all over the world.

Jerusalem: The city where *Baitul Muqaddas* is situated. *Baitul Muqaddas* is in the occupancy of the Israelis.

Hazrat Bal: It is a historical mosque in Srinagar Kashmir. It is situated on the bank of Dal Lake. Holy hair of the Prophet's (Pbuh) beard is kept here. People come here to see the holy hair on some occasions.

OIC. Organisation of Islamic Countries: Its Head Quarters are in Rabat, Morocco, Africa.

Index

Aab-e-kausar, 52
Acts of gross injustice, 151, 154
Adeeb Kamil, 129, 133
Aeronautical Engineering, 130
'Ahad', meaning of, 4
Ahl-e-Hadith, 38, 47, 49, 156
Ajmal Khan, 123
Alcohol, 85
Aligarh Muslim University, 135–36
American attack on Iraq, 111–14
Animalism, 88, 111, 146
Anti-India terrorists, 107
Anti-Muslim
  acts, 120
  forces, 103
  parties, 117
Anti-social elements, 93, 120
Aqsa Mosque, 66
Arab League, 114
Arabic language, 18, 42, 48, 53
Asr prayers, 156
Astrology, 87
Atrocities, 119
Aurangzeb, 66, 109–10
Ayodhya, 27, 50

Bank interest, 31
Barelvis, 73, 99–100, 157
Basic articles of faith, 35, 46, 49, 62, 67, 76
Bestial atrocities, 119
Birth control, 69, 87
BJP, 108, 117, 120–21, 124
Blood-money, 45
Brailawis, 37, 47, 67
Bribe, 85
Bride, 22, 70, 80–81, 95, 98
Bridegroom, 70, 80–81, 95, 97–98
Brotherhood, 7, 16, 27, 31, 34, 37, 57, 93, 99, 124, 146–47, 150
Burraq, 28, 156

Caliph of Islam, 52, 156
Canon of Islam, 6–7
Caste system, 53, 77, 81, 86, 100
Casteism, 98–99
Castration, 24
Catholic Christian, 140
Celestial ascension, 35, 58–59, 61, 66, 156
Charity, 21, 35, 61, 84, 89, 126, 157
Chastity, 70, 90–91
Chishti Sufi tradition, 68
Christianity, 19, 50–51
Circumcision, 23–24, 62
Classical poets, 140
Cleanliness, 5, 25, 27, 56, 70, 86, 157
Commodities, 70, 96
Communal
  harmony, 16, 21, 103
  riots, 89–90, 93, 144, 150, 154
  violence, 104, 114, 120, 125
Congregational prayer, 26
Congress Party, 116–17
Consensus, 2, 5, 26, 61, 63, 67, 73, 86, 93, 112, 115, 127
Constitution, 27, 80, 107–8, 112, 114, 118, 145, 150
Constitutional body, 149
Cow-slaughter, 74, 112
Creator, 29, 33, 37, 42, 51, 53, 55, 57, 59, 61, 69, 71, 145
Criminal laws, 67
Curfew, 143
Custody, 38

Daily prayers, 56–57, 64
Dalits, 100, 102, 109, 125
Darul Harb, 31
Darul Qaza, 94

Darul Uloom, 79, 103, 132, 135, 157
Day of Judgement, 41–42, 53, 65
Death punishment, 45
Death sentence, 2
Democratic country, 106, 119
Democratic traditions, 122–23
Deobani mosque, 62
Divorce, 12–14, 37, 69–70, 75, 81, 83, 89, 112, 155–56
Divorced woman, 12, 14, 155
Domestic animals, 97
Dowry, 80, 84
Dress code, 21
Drought, 95
Duty hours, 142

Eid-ul Azha, 1, 20, 38, 71
    animals sacrificial, 1
Electoral process, 120–21
Evil acts, 32, 56, 77

Fajr prayer, 3, 4, 9, 26
Family planning, 69
Fasting, 15–16, 19, 27, 32, 40, 52, 57, 144
Fatiha, 58, 155
Fatwa, 13, 72, 99
Female slaves, 89
Festivals, 7, 20
Financial help, 134
Fiqh, 54, 61, 115, 155
Fitr, 126
Five daily prayers, 2, 18, 21, 26–27, 29–31, 35, 40, 47–48, 52, 56, 61, 66, 90–91, 153, 156–57
Forgiveness, 7–8, 22, 30, 45–46, 72, 91
Freedom fighters, 123, 135
Freedom struggle, 134–35
Friday prayer, 7, 15–16, 43, 48–49
Fundamental beliefs, 47, 100
Fundamental teachings, 42, 87, 153
Funeral prayer, 2, 17, 41, 64–65

Genocide, 93
Ghair Muslim, 157
Glory of Allah, 19, 55
Graveyard, 9, 23, 68, 146
Gujarat riots, 114, 149
Gulf countries, 111, 113

Hadith, 9, 11, 14, 19, 23, 30–31, 34–35, 44–45, 48–49, 52–54, 60–62, 86–87, 89, 155, 157–58
Hadrat Adam, 26, 44
Hadrat Ibraheem, 50–51
Hajj, 6–9, 17, 30, 51, 57, 75, 90, 96, 100, 158
    meaning of, 7
    obligatory observances of, 7
    vs. Qurbani , 6
Hajj-e-Akbar, 6
Hajj-e-Asghar, 6
Halal, 71, 141, 155
Hanafi jurisprudence, 38
Haram, 9, 41, 71, 74, 96, 127, 155
Hazrat Ali, 80, 86, 156–57
Hazrat Ayyub, 73–74
Hazrat Bal, 53, 66, 158
Hazrat Daud, 65–66
Hazrat Ibraheem, 6–8, 10, 46, 59
Hazrat Ismaeel, 46
Hazrat Nizamuddin Auliya, 35, 54, 70, 121, 141–42
Head coverings, 5
Hero-worship, 104
Hijri, 32, 66, 143, 147, 149
Hindu Ethics and Indian Religion and Culture, 128
Hindu religion, 74
Hindu terrorism, 105, 110
Holy house of Allah, 6–7, 9, 30, 39, 46, 75, 90, 96, 158
House of Allah, 8, 39
Hypocrites, 62–63, 122, 157

Iddat, 12–14, 156
Idol worship, 10, 51, 53, 57, 70
Ihram, 5–6
Imam Husain, 10–11, 54, 158
India Muslim League, 108
India Muslim Personal Law, 115
India Personal Law Board, 13
Infiltrators, 106
Injunctions, 11
International Islamic conference, 103
Invocation of Allah, 17, 40
Irish Republican Army (IRA), 137, 140
Irreligious, 18, 37
ISI, 138
Islamic
    banks, 121
    beliefs, 4, 7–9, 11, 15–16, 18, 27, 29, 39, 41, 46, 51–52, 59–61, 64, 68, 87
    calendar, 12, 14, 158
    caliphate, 34
    code of dress, 75
    fiqh, 115
    fraternity, 7
    Jihad, 146–47
    jurisprudence, 6

laws, 13, 15, 19–22, 52, 73, 77, 80, 95–97, 155–56
mysticism, 155
revolution, 116, 119
way of life, 84, 148
Israel, 65–66, 113, 119, 122, 138

Jama Masjid, 78, 121, 123, 125, 151
Jamat-e-Islami, 99, 110–11, 118
Jamia Millia Islamia, 128, 131–34
Jan Sangh, 121
Jerusalem, 4, 65, 158
Jews, 24, 26, 29, 34, 38, 43, 65, 75, 158
Jihad, 31, 125, 139, 146, 151
Jinns, 53
Judaism, 50
Juma prayer, 2, 15, 23, 25

Kalima, 28–29, 58
Khan, Ashfaqulla, 106, 134
Khusrow, Amir, 141
Khwaja Moinuddin Chishti, 35, 66, 68

Land abolition act, 13
Last rituals, 91
Love-making, 4
Loyal Allah, 25

Madinah, 1, 6
Madrasas, 58, 95, 100, 119, 128–29, 131, 133–34, 138
Makkah, 1, 6
journey expenses, 6
Marriage, 12, 14–15, 17, 22, 29, 36, 51, 70, 73, 75, 80–85, 87, 89–90, 95–100, 157
bond of, 12–14, 78, 81, 83, 94, 138, 158
contract of, 14, 75
court, 99
intersect, 51
occasion of, 80
Martyrdom, 11, 20, 36, 158
Masjid-ul-Aqsa, 4
Massacre, 149–50
Menstrual period, 71, 75, 81–82
Messengers of Allah, 1, 4, 18, 46, 48
Milli Council, 99
Modi, Narender, 106
Moharram, 20, 36
Money lender, 126
Muhammadan Anglo Oriental College, 135–36
Muhammad-ur-Rasulallah, 29
Muharram, 54, 67, 158
Munkir-Nakeer, 60
Muqaddas, Baitul, 58, 61, 65–66, 158
Muslim Fiqh Academy, 115
Muslim Personal Law, 13, 115
Muslim Sufis, 35
Muslim thief, 2
Muslim Ulama, 112
Muslim voters, 120
Muslim worship houses, 147

Nadwatul Ulama, 131–32
Nafl prayers, 23, 28, 50
Namaz, 156
National Minority Commission, 145
National song, 144
Neutral Muslim pray, 62
Non-Muslim ancestors, 16
Non-Muslim students, 128
Non-obligatory prayer, 2
Non-vegetarians, 41, 104
Non-votary of prayer, 2
Numerals 786 , 5

Obligatory
duty, 6–7, 9, 29, 75, 139
observances, 7
prayer, 17
Oneness of Allah, 11, 35, 46–47, 155

Patriotism, 104, 106
Peace-loving countries, 111
Physical deformity, 24
Pilgrimage, 6–9, 30, 57, 75, 90, 96, 158
farewell, 46
free, 9
Pillars of Islam, 46, 84
Political party, 102, 108, 116, 120–21, 123
POTA, 111, 114, 120
Preferential treatment, 18
Pregnancy, 12, 69
Pre-Islamic ancestors, 154
Pro-Muslim parties, 124
Prophet Muhammad, 4, 6–8, 11, 15–20, 22–23, 26, 28–29, 39–40, 42, 48–49, 57–59, 61–66, 77, 89–90, 155–56
Prophet of Islam, 8
Prophethood, 1, 8, 41, 59
Prophetic traditions, 3–4, 8–9, 11–12, 17, 35, 43, 56, 59, 71, 73, 75, 77, 88, 136, 153–54
Punishment, 2–3, 22, 24, 33, 38, 40, 45, 91, 126, 149

Qazi Mujahidul Islam, 32, 115

Rabta Aalam-e-Islami, 32
Rabta-e-Islami Fiqh Academy, 32
Ragging, 81
Rajju Bhaiyya, 117–18
Ramazan, 16, 18–19, 62–63, 70
Religious
  advancement, 4
  balance, 100
  beliefs, 21, 57, 147
  biases, 37
  body, 148
  books, 105, 142, 146–47
  communities, 112, 119
  decree, 104
  diversity, 27
  education, 26, 104, 128, 131, 147
  faith, 112, 118
  fold, 74
  groups, 112, 124
  guide, 92
  issues, 155
  laws, 112
  liberty, 31
  practices, 46
  rights, 156
  rituals, 28, 56–57, 73, 156
  sanction, 99, 139
  sects, 139, 157
  sentiments, 76
  symbol, 9
  traditions, 50, 54, 56–57, 63, 142
  values, 147
  war, 139
Revelation of the Qur'an, 1, 30, 42
RSS, 117–18

Sacrifice, 10, 24, 46, 57, 64, 106, 112, 125, 136
Sacrificial animal, 1, 6, 11, 24, 27, 33, 35, 38, 49, 71, 157
Sacrificial offerings, 10
Sajda-e-Tazeemi, 36
Samajwadi Party, 124
Sang-e-Aswad, 8, 51
Saudi Arabia, 53, 158
Scholar of Islam, 31, 54
Sectarianism, 67, 100
Secular education, 26
Shab-e-Barat, 46
Shah Nama-e-Islam, 131
Shahi Imam, 123, 125
Shaikhul Islam, 102
Sharia, 13–14, 32–33, 46, 75, 78, 86, 97–98, 157
Shariat, 7, 20, 155
Shia Muslims, 98
Silk clothes, 96
SIMI, 111, 125
Sinful acts, 40, 72, 78, 89–90, 92, 96
Sir Syed Ahmad Khan, 35, 108, 112, 117, 136, 144
Skull caps, practice of wearing, 5
Slaughtered animals, 32, 141
Social duties, 22
Solar calendar, 143
State of anger, 11–12
Sterilisation, 30
Subsistence allowance, 13, 80
Sunnat prayer, 50
Sunnis, 14, 30, 47, 51, 59, 86, 98, 157
Supreme Court, 13, 80, 119–20
Surahs, 1, 3, 19–20, 50, 56, 62, 66–67, 155–56
Swami Dayananda Saraswati, 55–56

Tableeghi Jamaat, 36, 40, 58, 73
Tagore, Rabindra Nath, 144
Taj Mahal, 83
Talibanis, 79, 129
Terrorism, 45, 107, 119, 129, 140, 146, 148
Thick clots, 136
Traditional religious subjects, 132
Triple talaq, 11–14, 75, 99, 155
True Islam, 152

Uncleanliness, 27, 38
Uniform civil code, 112, 119–20
United Nations, 138
Urdu, 5, 49, 129–30, 133, 135, 138–42, 144, 147–48

Vande Matram, 142
Vibhuti Narain Rai, 154
Violence, 31, 114, 120, 137, 141
Vishva Hindu Parishad, 107–8, 114

Wahid, meaning of, 4
Wajd, 3
Witchcraft, 153–54
Worship, 4, 6, 8, 16, 28–29, 36, 47, 50, 52–53, 55, 59, 64–65, 131, 143, 156
Worshipful acts, 34, 48, 62, 90

Zakat, 21–22, 38, 57, 89, 95, 126–27
Zakir Hussain, 123, 130, 132
Zuhr prayer, 2, 15, 142
Zulaikha, 3
Zulqarnain, 25, 34